Constructing
Orientation to Mu ......g

Constructing a Personal Orientation to Music Teaching is a textbook for studies in music education. It promotes inquiry and reflection to facilitate teacher growth, lifelong learning, and a disposition toward educational change. In recent history many initiatives have sought to define what music teachers should know and be able to do. Teacher educators have attempted to build on such initiatives to structure and guide their programs. In these proposals the teacher's voice is often missing. This book ascribes to the notion of a personal orientation as a way to include, amplify, and situate the future teacher in the center of learning to teach.

Strongly grounded in current theories and research in teacher education, *Constructing a Personal Orientation to Music Teaching* strives to:

- Engage readers in analyzing their own experiences in order to conceptualize the complexity of teaching
- Involve them in clarifying their reasons for seeking a career in teaching
- Support their insights, questions, and reflections about their work
- Promote a reflective, critical attitude about schools in general as music teachers are urged to think of themselves as change agents in school settings.

Every chapter includes a wealth of pedagogical features, including exercises and problems that apply key ideas and concepts, first-person narratives that illustrate how personal experience influences thinking and action in teaching, summaries of relevant research studies in teacher education, and annotated reading lists.

Mark Robin Campbell is Associate Professor of Music Education at the Crane School of Music, State University of New York at Potsdam.

Linda K. Thompson is Associate Professor at the Lee University School of Music in Cleveland, Tennessee.

Janet R. Barrett is Associate Professor of Music Education at the Bienen School of Music at Northwestern University.

Constructing a Personal Orientation to Music Teaching

MARK ROBIN CAMPBELL
The Crane School of Music of the State University of
New York at Potsdam

LINDA K. THOMPSON
School of Music Lee University

JANET R. BARRETT
Bienen School of Music Northwestern University

Routledge
Taylor & Francis Group
NEW YORK AND LONDON

First published 2010
by Routledge
711 Third Avenue, New York, NY 10017, USA

Simultaneously published in the UK
by Routledge
2 Park Square, Milton Park, Abingdon, Oxon OX14 4RN

Routledge is an imprint of the Taylor & Francis Group, an informa business

Typeset in Minion and Helvetica Neue by Swales & Willis Ltd, Exeter, Devon

Library of Congress Cataloging-in-Publication Data
    Campbell, Mark Robin.
    Constructing a personal orientation to music teaching / Mark Robin Campbell,
    Linda K. Thompson, Janet R. Barrett.
      p. cm.
    Includes bibliographical references and index.
    1. Music teachers—Training of. 2. Music—Instruction and study.
    I. Thompson, Linda K. II. Barrett, Janet R. III. Title.
    MT3.U5C25 2011
    780.71—dc22
    2009052936

ISBN 13: 978–0–415–87183–9 (hbk)
ISBN 13: 978–0–415–87185–3 (pbk)
ISBN 13: 978–0–203–84879–1 (ebk)

Contents

Preface

Learning to teach is a lifelong endeavor. With our collective 93 years of teaching, we rediscover this truth each time we walk into a classroom. During these years we have been privileged to engage with hundreds of future music educators in our classes, and we have come to recognize that these students hold two things in common. They all bring their personal educational autobiographies and beliefs to bear on their experiences in music teacher education programs, and they all must find for themselves the teaching paths they will take both during and following their work as students in these programs. It is through exploring the first commonality that preservice teachers will begin to chart and pursue the second.

Our firmly held belief in the power and potential of exploring one's individual and personal experiences in order to make sense of the present and ultimately to shape future experiences has compelled us to write this book. We hold to the notion of a *personal orientation to music teacher preparation*, grounding teaching and learning in the personal, the practical, and the interactive, and placing the teacher–learner at the center of the educational process. Learning to teach is construed as an ongoing process of becoming. Key to this process is understanding the teacher's role as that of a lifelong learner, shaped by personal and professional inquiry. A powerful result of this inquiry is a professional identity of teacher-as-change-agent with a vision of the possible in music education.

Throughout this book opportunities are presented to develop preservice teachers' abilities to analyze past experiences in order to conceptualize for themselves the complexity of teaching. This autobiographical, narrative focus also promotes teachers' capacities to clarify their reasons for seeking a life in music teaching, and supports their insights, questions, and reflections about their work. At the same time, we seek to promote a reflective, critical attitude about schools in general as teachers are urged to think of themselves as change agents in school settings. In the current era of school reform, societal and cultural changes, and postmodern approaches to curriculum, teachers must be able to question past practices, astutely observe and analyze current practices, and creatively implement new innovations.

We are intentional in what we have chosen to include in this book, and in what we have omitted. You will find numerous opportunities to cultivate dispositions of teacher-as-lifelong-learner; you will not find traditional notions of teacher preparation as "training" with an emphasis on attainment of sets of discrete skills. You will find an emphasis on developing and nurturing a stance of inquiry related to professional and educational contexts—of continuous, systematic investigation into your educational past and present; you will not find the view of teaching as experts delivering pre-determined content, nor will you find an overview of typical music teaching structures and systems or attributes that define "successful" music programs. We do believe that teachers should be skilled and that teaching should be skillful, but we do not suggest specific ways to master a set of teaching techniques. Rather we see this text as a way to view music education and being a music teacher in a holistic manner.

We envision this book as a student's companion integrated throughout undergraduate and graduate music education programs. This book is not intended to be course specific. It has been designed for flexibility and can be used on an "as appropriate or needs be" basis throughout music education introductory courses, methods courses, practica, student teaching, and graduate work. Doctoral students may wish to use this not only to explore the text in relation to their own learning and professional growth, but in preparation for working with future music educators in years to come.

Throughout the book, the concept of developing a personal orientation to teaching and learning music is represented as a dynamic model. Core ideas embedded in a personal orientation are examined across multiple chapters and in various contexts (university classrooms, field sites and through self-reflection and interaction with a wide range of individuals involved in the music education profession). Strategies drawn from qualitative research methodologies (ethnographic techniques, narrative, reflection, case studies) provide a framework for inquiry.

Specific aspects unique to this text include:

> *Take Action* exercises and problems designed to engage preservice teachers in thinking about the implications and applications of key ideas and concepts;

> *At Close Range* segments relating first-person narratives collected from preservice and practicing teachers and focusing on chapter concepts, illustrating how personal experience influences thinking and action in teaching;

> *Focus On Research* sections summarizing relevant research studies in music teacher education with particular emphasis on implications for teaching and learning;

> *For Your Inquiry* annotations at the end of chapters, recommending readings to further extend the main ideas of the chapters.

Other distinctive features of the text include *Appendix 1: Ethics of Going Into The Field*, which addresses principles of and procedures for responsible research and inquiry. This appendix provides a corollary to the *Take Action* field experiences and data collection in schools. Additionally, the text reflects a strong grounding in current theories and research from within and outside the field of music teacher education, presented in a readable way with multiple opportunities for reflection.

To The Student: We invite you to think of this text as an opportunity to enter into, interact with, and reflect on ideas of music teaching and learning to teach. The *Take Action* exercises are self-, field- and people-oriented, and we encourage you to revisit these ideas and activities throughout your music teacher education program.

To The Professor: We encourage you to use this text throughout the music teacher education program with readings and activities integrated into existing course work. It provides the opportunity to challenge and develop students' thinking, and it also serves to provide coherence across courses and field experiences. *Take Action* exercises can be easily adapted for graduate students currently teaching, and doctoral students may find this enriching for themselves personally as well as for use with their future students. This book has been specifically designed to work within all of the professional development courses found in accredited music education degree programs. It may be used chapter-by-chapter, or section-by-section, and certain aspects and ideas may be revisited repeatedly throughout the music education program. *Appendix 2: How To Use This Book* provides specific suggestions on how different features of the text could be used within specific courses or across an entire music teacher education program.

This book would not be possible without the inspiration and help from many people. We would like to thank the students from each of our collective years of teaching who have acted as "informants" and provided "rich and thick" data for contemplation, as well as many opportunities for personal reflections. We would especially like to thank the following former students, who have specifically contributed to the contents of this book: Ted Ehnle, Kate Fitzpatrick, Phillip Greco, Jennifer Horn, Melissa Natale-Abramo, and Jeff Nelson. Jennifer Shuck provided invaluable assistance in preparing the manuscript. Michael Leuze's technological skills also contributed to the final stages of manuscript preparation.

Lastly, we would like to acknowledge the powerful influences of our own teachers and mentors: Eunice Boardman, Richard Colwell, Charles Leonhard, Dorothy McDonald, Stephen J. Paul, and Marilyn Zimmerman.

Mark Robin Campbell
Linda K. Thompson
Janet R. Barrett
October 2009

one
Starting the Journey

Developing a Personal View of Teaching and Learning

Purposes, interests, and meanings constitute the underlying facts of human experience.
Lewis Mumford "Orientation to Life," *The Conduct of Life,* 1951

Life is a succession of events which must be lived to be understood.
Ralph Waldo Emerson "Illusions," *The Conduct of Life,* 1860, rev. 1876

FOCUS
In this chapter we invite you to consider your own histories as learners and develop your identities as teachers. Our aim is to engage you in the process of constructing a personal view of teaching and learning through writing and reflecting on a wide range of experiences.

Getting Started

Each of you has a story to tell about how or why you got interested in teaching or how you became involved in the world of music. Many music teachers are drawn to a life of teaching because they have a genuine love of music, a deep concern for others, and a strong desire to "pass along" the joy of music to others. In fact, experienced music teachers—those with at least 15 years of teaching—say that being shown how they have affected the life of a student has been a positive and career changing event in their teaching (Cutietta & Thompson, 2000).

Music teachers are hopeful that a new generation of young people will have opportunities to participate in many different kinds of musical offerings and come to appreciate the varied musical activities of those around them. Music teachers are also eager to learn about others—their interests and desires—as well as to teach from a solid base of musical understanding. The majority of music teachers, however, realize that there is more to teaching music than the simple transmission of a teacher's knowledge and musical skills to another less knowledgeable or less skilled other. Rather, to paraphrase Seymour Sarason, music teachers know that the stuff we traditionally call music—the activities, facts, skills and concepts that make up the subject matter—only attains meaning when teaching processes take into account the "child's curiosity, interests, conceptual level, and need to act on the world" (1993, p. 242). In other words, we not only teach music, we teach people.

Personal Influences

Although these generalities about what music educators value in teaching are important, it is also important to look at the particularities of how you have come to be where you are in your life. What has influenced your decision to be a music teacher? As Eunice Boardman (1992) notes, no mind is a blank slate when it comes to what we believe is good music teaching. That is, each of us comes to teaching with a personal perspective—a stage, so to speak, on which we build our understanding of the way the world is. Whether our beliefs remain unexamined or have been explicitly articulated, our personal perspective forms the basis on which we justify, make sense of, and unify our actions and thoughts. In addition, the beliefs, expectations, ideals, and influences of others also inform our perspective. Collectively, our experiences function as filters in building our images of teaching and learning.

There are many stories that deserve telling and many stories that we can share that will help us make sense of learning to teach, especially if we use a framework that allows us to look at the teaching and learning process as a multidimensional phenomenon. A personal orientation to music teaching and learning looks at all participants in the educational process from a dynamic perspective. That is, as we continue to deepen and extend our knowledge of self and others, it is always in the service of more and better teaching. We are not only present oriented; we are also past and future oriented in our thinking about teaching. Most importantly, a personal orientation framework helps us to understand ourselves; it helps us to understand the music experiences we value, the places and situations that support learning, and the ways we can help others. Think about the influential people in your life who have made an impact on your decision to teach music. Also, think about influential experiences and events that have occurred in your life that may have contributed to your decision to becoming a music teacher. Take a few moments to read Erica's story, which she composed as an introduction to her student teaching supervisor.

AT CLOSE RANGE 1.1
Erica: Taking Stock and Looking Forward

I was a sophomore in high school when I seriously entertained the idea of being a music teacher. Prior to that, I knew I wanted to teach from the moment I stepped into third grade. It was the job I knew I wanted to do and it stuck with me throughout the rest of my education.

I began music at the age of five. For me, reading music came right after I began reading English; it was all second nature. My first instrument was the "mother-mandated" piano. I took private lessons from ages five to eleven, taking from two different teachers. The clarinet, a choice that I made when I was nine, slowly took first place in my heart. After six years of piano, I decided I didn't have enough time to devote to both instruments so I narrowed my musical interests focusing strictly on the clarinet.

Between fifth and eleventh grades, I slowly honed my clarinet skills. I participated in numerous All-County and Area All-State ensembles, solo festivals, honors youth orchestras and countless musical activities within my school and community. While I was in high school, I also learned to sing and play the saxophone. I joined the choir and jazz band and, by this time, made the decision that I wanted to have music in the rest of my life. I should add that I spend a considerable amount of time listening to music and must confess that I have a fondness for jazz— owning many recordings of Miles Davis and Monk. When the application process came around and it became time to think seriously about going to college and choosing a career, I decided to pursue a degree in Music Education. The School of Music was my first choice, partly because I had gone to camp there as a teenager, and also because I had wonderful teacher-mentors who completed their studies there.

In preparing for the application process, I wrote countless essays, explaining who I was and what my fortes were in music. I always mentioned that I was a strong sight-reader, played with strong emotion, worked like a dog in the practice room, aimed to improve my clarinet technique and facility, and had years of experience teaching private lessons. My goals now are to create lessons that capture young children's attention and make a difference in their lives. I hope to draw upon my strong interpersonal skills and my sense of compassion when I work with them. I want to make sure that I get on their level. What I'm currently lacking is the ability to create a magnificent musical learning environment and the practical skills that you learn from practice teaching, plus the flair and energy to make things challenging for all students, but not so challenging as to go over their heads.

I have had a lot of experience with elementary school students, having taught beginning saxophone lessons and early intermediate clarinet lessons while in high school. I feel I have a good grasp on how children act at certain ages and what they know. From my observations, I know that all children need to be actively engaged to be learning. I look forward to working with children more closely and being more careful in developing an understanding of how they learn. I hope to find out what excites them and then tap into that in order to make learning engaging.

Where I'm afraid I lack the most confidence is in classroom management and lesson plan design. These are two areas of teaching where my thinking is tentative, partially because they set the mood of the classroom and they denote what is taken away from the class. If the lesson plans aren't well constructed, the students aren't able to pull as much from the lesson as what they could have. Even though I may have all the training and ideas in the world, I still feel unprepared and still won't be able to assess how good I am until I am out there, presenting my lesson in front of my class. What I do know is that children are excited if you are; they need to be treated as equals and never looked down upon. In addition, I am leery about integrating the national standards for music education, as they still befuddle me at times.

All in all, I am ready to take on student teaching. I look forward to trying out "new" ideas on my "students" and seeing how a classroom really works.

What does Erica's story reveal about the different influences on her decision to become a music teacher? One of the primary influences in Erica's story is the presence of various important people. They were a strong force in her life and had a powerful impact on her growth as a music maker—her mother, and several different music teachers. Another strong influence in Erica's story is the music itself. Her story tells us something about the ways in which we interact with music—playing and singing and listening—and the values we attach to their importance (See Woodford, 2005). It also shows how one musical endeavor may lead to another—developing skills and acquiring new knowledge across different but related musical contexts. Clearly Erica's involvement in playing and learning to play new instruments creates a sense of the intensity she attaches to music involvement. Erica's story reveals much about her thinking in relation to teaching and learning music. Her prior work with students, her observations of classrooms, and her knowledge of lesson planning have led her to believe in certain ways of working with learners. Her belief that active engagement is an important part of learning will likely influence the ways she judges her success as a teacher, and the manner in which she works with students (See Bergee & Grashel, 2002). We don't know or can't tell from Erica's story, however, what "actively engaged" learning means or even looks like. So this area of Erica's story remains "open" and ready for further investigation. The whole idea is likely to change or at least become more refined in its articulation as she gains more experience working with learners and reflecting on her interactions with them.

Whether or not we are aware of our personal history, it has a significant impact on our thinking about the present and the future. In thinking about your own history as a learner and the influences that have contributed to your thinking about music, teaching and learning, take a few moments to engage in the following set of exercises which we call "Take Action."

TAKE ACTION 1.1
Connecting to the Past—Powerful Experiences as a Learner

Often thinking about learning tells us much about teaching and what may be guiding us in our own beliefs about teaching. The purpose of this exercise is to help you reflect on the impact of learning experiences in your own educational history.

- Think about two or three powerful learning experiences that you have had.
- Write them down. Indicate the context (where they occurred) and the amount of time involved. Describe each experience using as much detail as you are able.
- Analyze each of your experiences, indicating what was significant or powerful about each one. To develop and expand your analysis you may want to write about who was involved and what happened to bring about learning. Or, include what was being learned and why or if it seemed special. There may also be something distinctive about the experience; discuss that. Lastly, indicate how you felt.

When you begin to think about writing about your powerful learning experiences, don't feel compelled to limit yourself to those you remember only from being in school. Music education philosopher and educator Estelle Jorgensen (1997) tells us that there are many "spheres of validity" through which meaning is constructed and the manner in which we make sense of things (p. 37). Here are some additional people and places to consider:

- Home—family, parents, siblings, relatives
- Religious events or groups—organizations, worship
- Work environments—boss, peers, customers
- Schools—teachers, other students, projects
- Social groups—clubs, sports teams, dramatics
- Music Profession—professional, amateur musicians
- Friends—events, specific persons—older, younger

TAKE ACTION 1.2
Connecting to the Past—Powerful Experiences with Music

In their book, *Sound Ways of Knowing* (1997), Janet Barrett, Claire McCoy and Kari Veblen ask music education students to engage in an exercise designed to help them think about their personal musical experiences and the ways these experiences affect their lives. On an unlined sheet of paper, draw circles to show different pools of musical activity in your personal history: your "music circles" diagram. The categories listed below may be helpful to get you started, but feel free to add additional categories to the list. Label each circle with the category title inside each circle and jot down the titles or short descriptions of the music that fits within the category. Because some of the circles may be related in time or place, you might want to make them appear close together or overlapping on your diagram. Others may stand alone as singular events.

- Early memories—songs you remember being sung to you as a child
- Songs you recall singing in school
- Musical works you have performed
- Songs you can sing or pieces you can play entirely from memory
- Recordings you would not want to live without
- Your least favorite music examples
- Music you have heard or performed in the past 24 hours
- Music you have taught (or love to teach) to others
- Music that puzzles you, intrigues you, challenges you
- Hidden pleasures—what others might be surprised to know about your tastes.

When you have completed drawing and labeling your circles, contemplate what they reveal about your musical interests and involvement. In what ways do these circles reflect the influences of the time and place you were born, places you've lived, and significant people in your life? Figures 1.1, 1.2 and 1.3 show three different sets of circles representing three preservice teachers: *Kara, Brett* and *Don*.

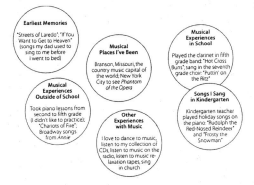

FIGURE 1.1. Kara's Music Circles.
From Janet R. Barrett, Claire W. McCoy, & Kari K. Veblen, *Sound Ways of Knowing*, New York: Schirmer Books, 1997; Reprinted with permission from Janet R. Barrett, Copyrighted © 2009, all rights reserved.

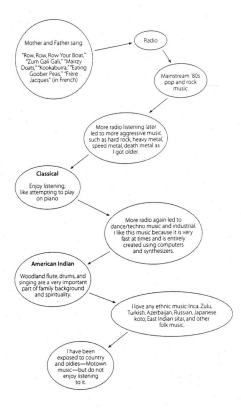

FIGURE 1.2. Brett's Music Circles.
From Janet R. Barrett, Claire W. McCoy, & Kari K. Veblen, *Sound Ways of Knowing*, New York: Schirmer Books, 1997; Reprinted with permission from Janet R. Barrett, Copyrighted © 2009, all rights reserved.

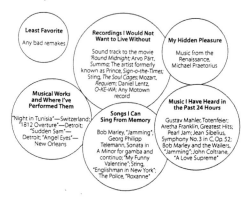

FIGURE 1.3. Don's Music Circles.
From Janet R. Barrett, Claire W. McCoy, & Kari K. Veblen, *Sound Ways of Knowing*, New York: Schirmer Books, 1997; Reprinted with permission from Janet R. Barrett, Copyrighted © 2009, all rights reserved.

TAKE ACTION 1.3
Connecting to the Past—Chronology of Educational Musical Experience

The purpose of this Take Action is to help you construct a biographical time-line that identifies the important musical and educational events that influenced your decision to become a teacher.

- Create a timeline that lists important musical and educational events that were personally significant to you.
- Describe these events and explain why they were important or how they had an influence on your decision to become a teacher.
- Compare your timeline with a classmate or get together with a small group from class. Are there any commonalities across each person's time-line? What seems distinctive among everyone's timeline? Try constructing category themes using the group's set of timelines. Look for common characteristics that might be organized into groups or categories of ideas. For example, each timeline might mention one or two individuals who played seminal roles in your decision to become a teacher. If so, you might create a larger category called "Significant People or Role Models."
- Share your analysis with others.

Impact of Personal History on Teaching

So far, you have been encouraged to think about different influences that have made an impact on you as a learner. You have also examined your musical background, and have constructed a timeline that highlights important events and experiences in your life. What insights have you gained so far? What have the exercises revealed about what you value? Are there some kinds of musical experiences that seem to characterize your personal history more so than others? Were there some people who figured prominently in your background? Were there any points of intersection between your experiences as a learner, your musical background, and significant people? We hope that you are in a stronger position to see how individuals' personal histories have an impact on their thinking about teaching. Perhaps you might be able to see how your own identity as a music teacher has been shaped, and is likely to be shaped in the future. You may now be able to identify where you picked up certain attitudes and beliefs about teaching.

The process of how individuals acquire certain beliefs, values and mores or how they learn the rules and expectations of a group or a specific community is often explained as socialization. In its most simple definition, the process of socialization is seen as an ongoing assimilation and integration of life experiences whereby an individual adopts the norms, values and shared beliefs of a particular group in order to function within a specific environment or culture. Socialization is a lifelong process that begins at birth and occurs both explicitly and implicitly. That is, socialization occurs through direct instruction by others and by your own membership in a group. By being members of a group, individuals "pick up" what they perceive to be of value in the group and construct an identity that is congruent with the "way of life" in that group or within a particular society. Primary agents in the socialization process include your family, friends and peer group. Institutions such as schools, religious organizations and clubs also influence your self concept, emotions, attitudes and behaviors. Other influential agents in the socialization process include the mass media and the Internet. Pause to think about how certain socialization processes have created who you are, what you believe, how you act, and how you define teaching. Without much effort, you can probably provide fairly clear examples of how musical socialization functions in high schools, in drum and bugle corps, or in a music conservatory.

FOCUS ON RESEARCH 1.1
Influences on Collegiate Students' Decisions to Become a Music Educator

Martin Bergee and his associates (Bergee, Coffman, Demorest, Humphreys & Thornton, 2001) wanted to collect information on influences critical to collegiate music educators' decisions to pursue music teaching as a career. In collecting that information they designed a survey and systematically analyzed responses from college students who were members of their respective collegiate MENC chapters. They focused their research efforts on identifying the persons, experiences, events, organizations, and other factors that influenced the college students' decisions to teach music. Table 1.1 summarizes the major findings from their study.

TABLE 1.1 Influences on Becoming a Music Educator

Factor	Finding
When Decision Was Made	The majority (62%) of respondents indicated that their decision to become a music teacher was made in high school. Almost one-quarter made the decision while in college, and an additional 14% as early as their elementary years.
Influential Persons	High school ensemble directors and parents were indicated as strongly influential.
	The influence of private music teachers was high, as was the influence ascribed to professional musicians.
	Higher education music faculty members were most influential to those making the decision in the collegiate years.
Influential Experiences and Events	School experiences were seen to be most influential, with honors events/experiences a close second. Among critical events were participation in festivals and camps sponsored by higher education institutions.
Opportunities to Teach and Influence of Teaching Opportunities	When opportunities to teach were provided, over half (56%) of students who had taught indicated that those opportunities were either a "significant" or "very strong" influence.
Other Influential Factors	A deep devotion to music. Respondents overwhelmingly indicated a love of music as one of their primary motivating factors.

Looking at the Past and Seeing into the Future— What Makes a Successful Teacher?

Research by Dan Lortie (2002) has found that by the time you reach college, you have spent from 13,000 to 15,000 hours as an "apprentice of observing" successful and unsuccessful teaching. As we have noted previously, all of your past learning experiences have strongly affected your current views of what constitutes a significant learning experience. Each of you has a vision of a good teacher or has a story to share about an exceptional teacher in your life. When we have asked some of our own students (Campbell & Burdell, 1996; Campbell & Thompson, 2001) what they think characterizes good teachers, invariably we hear that teachers make learning fun, they like students, they love music, and know how to share it with others. It is the affective qualities of teachers that our students seem to remember most (Thompson, 2000). Rarely, however, do our students mention ideas that have to do with teaching strategies, explaining or demonstrating musical concepts, or assessing learners' skills, attitudes or knowledge. Nor do they mention more general types of pedagogical skills and knowledge, such as the ability to plan effectively for diverse learners, or the characteristics or needs of different types and ages of learners. Occasionally, however, students will mention teachers' involvements in special events that relate to curricular concerns. Like the students in the Collegiate MENC survey, our students almost always mention the role a teacher played in their participation in festivals, contests, and camps. In thinking about the influences that are likely to have contributed strongly to your conceptions about teaching, George J. Posner (2004) suggests that it is important for future teachers to think about their most successful *and* their most unsuccessful teachers. The ideas found in Take Action 1.4 and 1.5 are based on Posner's exercises for uncovering some of the assumptions under which beginning teachers may be operating when it comes to their beliefs about what makes a successful teacher.

TAKE ACTION 1.4
Successful Teacher/Unsuccessful Teacher

It is highly likely that a great many of your ideas about teaching and learning come from the teachers who you thought were successful in some way. The purpose of this exercise is to help you think about those teachers. Write a short teacher profile. The ideas listed below might be useful in getting started.

- Identify the most successful schoolteacher you have had.
- Write his or her name and some identifying preliminary characteristics that come immediately to mind.
- What seems to characterize the way this teacher worked with students?
- How did this teacher address the characteristics or needs of different types of learners?
- How did this teacher structure subject matter learning so that students could understand concepts and skills? Were there any special teaching strategies used that seem to be effective for your learning?
- How did this teacher assess learning? What specific strategies did s/he use that you thought were effective?
- What values do you think this teacher had in regard to schooling, student learning, and the community in which s/he worked?
- In the face of conflicts, or times of frustration, what do you believe sustained this teacher in the work he or she did?

After you have written your narrative of this successful teacher, make a list of characteristics that seem to "define" a successful teacher. After you have generated your list of characteristics, rewrite them in ways that define a successful teacher in general.

Sometimes it is helpful to look back into our pasts and think about teachers who seemed rather *unsuccessful.* Articulating what we think is unsuccessful can help clarify our ideas about what seems important to us. Write a short profile of this teacher. The ideas listed below might be useful in getting started.

- Identify an unsuccessful schoolteacher you have had. No need to write his or her name, just sketch out some identifying characteristics.
- What seemed to characterize the way this teacher worked with students?
- How did this teacher structure subject matter learning? Assess student understanding?
- Do you think this teacher was unsuccessful with other learners? Was there something distinctive in your relationship with this teacher?
- How do you think this teacher ended up being so unsuccessful?

Personal Teaching Metaphor

In our work with helping preservice music education teachers examine their personal musical and educational histories, we have often turned to the use of metaphor as a powerful device for shedding light on their own self-understanding, knowledge development, and personal orientations toward teaching. When you think about it, metaphors are pervasive in our thinking and conversations with others. Our daily language is filled with metaphor. Consider, for example, the implied meaning of such statements as "what a rat race," "spending time," or "pulling for the underdog." Consider also how metaphor can give meaning to ideas about the self. For example, a statement such as "I am the captain of my soul" implies both "sense of self" and a sense of agency—that is, a means by which we may produce effects. Metaphors are also representations of embodied experiences, and as such play an important role in the formation of teachers' ideals. Metaphors can also act as a bridge between our own individual images and narratives and help establish shared meanings with others (Bullough & Stokes, 1994). As George Lakoff and Mark Johnson (1980) note, metaphor helps us make sense of our worlds. Read the summary of a study designed to explore a group of preservice music educators' personal teaching metaphors. Once you have read through the study, complete Take Action 1.6.

FOCUS ON RESEARCH 1.2
Gods, Guides, and Gardeners: Preservice Music Educators' Personal Teaching Metaphors

Linda K. Thompson and Mark Robin Campbell (2005) were interested in exploring the use of metaphor in preservice teachers' representations of themselves as teachers and their relationships to conceptions of practice. Specifically, they sought to identify through self-generated pictorial and narrative metaphors the teaching roles and assumptions that preservice music teachers use to characterize themselves. The main study questions were: What do preservice music educators imagine teaching to be? What representations do they use to characterize teachers?

To carry out the study, Thompson and Campbell asked 99 preservice music educators who were enrolled in their first music education course at a School of Music to construct a metaphorical representation of themselves as teachers. Each student was specifically asked to:

- Draw a picture of an image of himself or herself as teacher.
- Label or title the picture "A teacher is like..." or "Teacher as..."
- Write a short paragraph describing what the picture intended to show.

To analyze the information the students provided, the researchers used a qualitative approach that included:

- Examining each student's response independently and then together.
- Constructing a category-classification scheme that compared and contrasted responses based upon patterns found among and across the students' responses.

Analysis of preservice music educators' pictorial and narrative metaphors indicated a wide range of responses with two broad categories that emerged for describing teaching roles and practice.

- Knowledge-based roles that clustered around ideas associated with teacher as transmitter, facilitator, and/or collaborator.
- Relationship-based roles that characterized student–teacher interactions around ideas associated with teacher as mentor, motivator, and/or leader.

Drawing upon the curricular work of Herbert Kliebard (1972), Thompson and Campbell suggested that three root metaphors could be employed in thinking about the teaching and learning processes on which the preservice music educators' personal teaching metaphors were based:

Production. Production metaphors characterize teachers as expert, skilled technicians whose goal is to "transmit" objectified and hierarchically classified bodies of knowledge to their students. Listening, recitation and rehearsal are seen as primary instructional processes for acquiring knowledge and skills. Efficiency and control are viewed as desirable qualities within the transmission process. The dominant teaching image is authoritarian and authority-based.

Growth. Growth metaphors characterize teachers as "laborers" whose goal is to bring about personal change in students. By creating "nurturing environments" and building strong student–teacher relationships, students are challenged to discover and reflect upon their experiences within a subject matter in order to develop their own understandings. No single teaching image adequately covers the dimensions of the growth metaphor. Facilitator, collaborator, mentor, and manager, however, capture various facets.

Travel. Travel metaphors characterize teachers as "guides" whose goal is to lead students through different "terrains" rich in knowledge, skills, attitudes, and appreciations. Student learning is dependent upon interest, intellectual development, social context, and teacher–student dialogue and inquiry, with the teacher pointing out or directing students' attention to important ideas for engagement. Images connected with the roles of leaders, directors, facilitators, collaborators, as well as transmitters or masters in a master–apprentice type of relation convey various aspects of being a guide.

TAKE ACTION 1.5
Teaching is Like …

This Take Action asks you to create an initial personal teaching metaphor in order to gain a window onto some of the assumptions that may be operating in your thinking.

- As a first step in developing your own teaching metaphor, reflect on images that you would use to characterize yourself as teacher. Also, take some time to imagine a context for your personal teacher images—that is, imagine what circumstances, events, or situations need to be present to create an environment that supports your images or enables you to enact your thoughts.
- Now place your images in a specific classroom context—What are you doing? What are the students doing? What is in the classroom that

contributes to your and the students' actions? What does the classroom feel like?

- Make a sketch of what is in your mind's eye, including your self, students, and the classroom context. Don't worry about the quality of your sketch, just get down everything you need to make your images and actions as detailed as possible.
- Label your sketch by identifying a metaphor that captures the core of your self as a teacher. Or provide a caption to your sketch that uses the following prompt: "Teaching is like …" or "Teacher as …"
- To help you generate your metaphor, recall that a metaphor is "giving one thing a name that belongs to something else."

A Framework For Thinking about Teaching and Learning: Teacher Standards

The teaching profession has a long history of trying to articulate what good teaching is and to distinguish excellent teachers from incompetent ones. The quest for indicators of successful teaching has been going on since at least 1870 when the National Education Association established the Department of Normal Schools. The New Teacher Assessment and Support Consortium (INTASC) and the National Board of Professional Teaching Standards (NBPTS) are currently two national organizations that have identified what they believe are essential characteristics of good and effective teachers. The INTASC standards are focused primarily on the preparation phase of learning to teach, while the NBPTS standards are designed for currently practicing teachers.

Of immediate interest to preservice music education teachers may be the INTASC standards. Many college and university teacher education programs use the INTASC standards as a common licensing framework for describing what competent beginning teachers need to know and be able to do in their first teaching positions. The standards also serve as a quality control mechanism that State Education Departments use when university teacher education programs seek official approval or accreditation from the state. In all likelihood, the institution that you are attending has a set of teacher standards that it uses to characterize or describe desired teacher qualities. However, when applied to the work of teacher educators, teacher standards can be used for both program planning and evaluation. When applied to your own education as preservice students, the teacher standards have varying degrees of relevance. What may be of most importance is their vision of practice, their articulations of sets of understanding about teaching, learning, and children, and their statements about dispositions required to use knowledge. Table 1.2 shows the Teacher Standards for INTASC, and Table 1.3 shows the Teacher Standards for NBPTS. As you read through both sets of standards, what

TABLE 1.2 The Interstate New Teacher Assessment and Support Consortium (INTASC) Teacher Standards

The Interstate New Teacher Assessment and Support Consortium (INTASC) is a group of state education agencies and national educational organizations dedicated to the reform of the preparation, licensing, and ongoing professional development of teachers. Created in 1987, INTASC's primary constituency is state education agencies responsible for teacher licensing, program approval, and professional development. Its work is guided by one basic premise: An effective teacher must be able to integrate content knowledge with the specific strengths and needs of students to assure that all students learn and perform at high levels.

INTASC Principles (Standards)

Principle #1: The teacher understands the central concepts, tools of inquiry, and structures of the discipline(s) he or she teaches and can create learning experiences that make these aspects of subject matter meaningful for students.

Principle #2: The teacher understands how children learn and develop, and can provide learning opportunities that support their intellectual, social and personal development.

Principle #3: The teacher understands how students differ in their approaches to learning and creates instructional opportunities that are adapted to diverse learners.

Principle #4: The teacher understands and uses a variety of instructional strategies to encourage students' development of critical thinking, problem solving, and performance skills.

Principle #5: The teacher uses an understanding of individual and group motivation and behavior to create a learning environment that encourages positive social interaction, active engagement in learning, and self-motivation.

Principle #6: The teacher uses knowledge of effective verbal, nonverbal, and media communication techniques to foster active inquiry, collaboration, and supportive interaction in the classroom.

Principle #7: The teacher plans instruction based upon knowledge of subject matter, students, the community, and curriculum goals.

Principle #8: The teacher understands and uses formal and informal assessment strategies to evaluate and ensure the continuous intellectual, social and physical development of the learner.

Principle #9: The teacher is a reflective practitioner who continually evaluates the effects of his/her choices and actions on others (students, parents, and other professionals in the learning community) and who actively seeks out opportunities to grow professionally.

Principle #10: The teacher fosters relationships with school colleagues, parents, and agencies in the larger community to support students' learning and well-being.

Note: Compiled from *Model standards for beginning teacher licensing, assessment and development: A resource for state dialogue.* Interstate New Teacher Assessment & Support Consortium, 1992. Available from: http://www.ccsso.org/projects/Interstate_New_Teacher_Assessment_and_Support_Consortium/ Accessed 5/30/2007.

TABLE 1.3 The National Board of Professional Teaching Standards (NBPTS)

The National Board of Professional Teaching Standards (NBPTS) is an independent, nonprofit, nonpartisan organization governed by a board of directors, the majority of whom are classroom teachers. Other members include school administrators, school board leaders, governors and state legislators, higher education officials, teacher union leaders and business and community leaders. The success of the National Board came from the power of a good idea: Quality teachers are necessary for student learning. The following standards are for practicing music teachers, those already certified and in the field.

Music Standards

I. Knowledge of Students
Accomplished music teachers understand the cognitive, physical, and social development of students and know their musical background; they use this knowledge to foster productive relationships with students and to provide music instruction that meets their needs.

II. Knowledge of and Skills in Music
Accomplished music teachers consistently demonstrate outstanding performance and musicianship skills; comprehensive knowledge of music theory and history; and highly specialized knowledge in general, choral, or instrumental music as they provide students with high-quality, sequential instruction in music.

III. Planning and Implementing Assessment
Accomplished music teachers plan and implement assessments, use assessment data in planning subsequent instruction, and employ a variety of methods to evaluate and report student progress.

IV. Facilitating Music Learning
Accomplished music teachers employ materials, methods, and strategies that engage students' interest and facilitate music learning. They have highly specialized knowledge in choral, instrumental, or general music as they provide students with high-quality, sequential instruction in music.

V. Learning Environments
Accomplished music teachers create and foster dynamic learning environments that are characterized by trust, risk taking, independence, collaboration, and high expectations for all students.

VI. Valuing Diversity
Accomplished music teachers value the diverse backgrounds, abilities, and perspectives of their students and provide a music curriculum that is inclusive of all students and rich in musical diversity.

VII. Collaboration
Accomplished music teachers understand and value the distinctive role of families, colleagues, the community, and others in the music education process and continually seek opportunities to build partnerships with them.

VIII. Reflection, Professional Growth, and Professional Contribution
Accomplished music teachers reflect on their teaching, students' performances, and developments in their field to extend their knowledge steadily, improve their teaching, and refine their philosophy of music education; they contribute to the growth of their colleagues, their schools, and their field.

Note: Complied from the *NBPTS music standards for teachers of students ages 3-18+*. National Board of Professional Teaching Standards, 2001. Available from: http://www.nbpts.org/about_us Accessed 5/30/2007.

themes related to learning, to knowledge, to dispositions can you draw out? How do the teacher standards compare to your own experiences of what makes an excellent teacher? Do you see any of the characteristics listed in the INTASC or NBPTS teacher standards present in the profile you constructed of "A Successful Teacher" in Take Action 1.4? Did your profile have qualities that the two national organizations did not?

Your Personal Perspective of Teaching: An Initial Perspective

Now that you have analyzed and compared the two sets of national teacher standards with your own profile of a successful teacher, what conclusions can you draw about teaching and learning? Teacher educator and researcher James Raths has suggested that the pursuit to distinguish competent teachers from incompetent ones is a "noble enterprise" (1999, p. 142). How would you characterize the efforts of the national teacher standards enterprise?

In this chapter we have encouraged you to begin the process of constructing a personal view of teaching and learning. We asked you to examine your personal educational and musical biographies to identify the ways your personal history affects your current thinking about teaching and music. We have also asked you to identify people in your lives who have influenced your decision to become a music teacher. In addition, you have looked at what you believe to be successful teaching and contrasted that with unsuccessful teaching. We have suggested that creating a personal teaching metaphor can help you explore and analyze your inner self, as well as reveal a more sophisticated understanding of some assumptions that may be implicit in your thinking about students. You have also had the opportunity to examine what different professional bodies imagine good teaching to be and compare them to your own images of good teaching. In closing this chapter, we ask you to synthesize the ideas you have uncovered. In this last Take Action, articulate your own personal perspective of teaching and learning.

TAKE ACTION 1.6
A Personal Perspective on Teaching and Learning

Me as Teacher

Look over each Take Action completed so far in Chapter 1. Create a representation of your self as teacher. Consider all of the influences on your decisions to become a teacher and how they affected your thinking. Think about your musical experiences and how they have contributed to your view of teaching and learning. You may also want to identify a significant event or

---

experience that had an affect on your decision to become a teacher or on the way you view teaching and learning. Your representation of yourself as a teacher can take any form. A written report or narrative is a traditional approach. However, do not feel limited to that. Use your imagination— poetry, song, collage, reader's theatre, multimedia—any of these can be used to express your perspective.

So What?

Understanding ourselves as teachers is enhanced when we articulate the *purposes* and *interests* that are likely to emerge from our representations of self. We can all construct an image of who we want to be as teachers, but what does this mean? Consider the following questions. They may help you reflect on the implications of forming a particular teacher image.

- What does your teacher image mean in terms of the people you will be working with? What does it mean for the different learners you encounter?
- What relationship does your teacher image have to the decisions you might make regarding materials or pieces of music used in the classroom?
- What does your personal perspective tell you about what you value in teaching and learning?
- What teaching skills and knowledge do you think are necessary in order for you to bring about learning, given the teacher you envision?
- What challenges do you see that might interfere with you becoming the teacher you envision?

To conclude, summarize what you believe the implications of your teacher image holds for you and the interactions you will have with:

- Learners
- Subject matter
- Working within a specific educational context.

We began this chapter with two quotes, both of which focused your thinking on the importance of experience, and how experience provides purpose, interest, and meaning in our lives. In the next chapter, we look at teaching as a career experience. Included here is an overview of various concerns and pathways that influence a teacher's career, as well as important events, opportunities, challenges and areas of professional development that give meaning to their practice.

For Your Inquiry

Ayers, W. (2001). *To teach: The journey of a teacher*. New York, NY: Teachers College Press.

To Teach is William Ayers' fascinating account of his own journey into the intellectual, moral and ethical worlds of teaching. As a provocative tale of things that actually happen in classrooms and within the broader world of education, Ayers "tells it as it is" with "no holds barred." Yet, as Gloria Ladson-Billings notes in the preface, Ayers does not "lead us to a place of hopelessness, powerlessness, or despair" (p. x). Rather, Ayers' sensitivity to the challenges facing teachers along with his practical suggestions for addressing those challenges act as an inspirational invitation to teachers at all stages of their careers. This book is for those practicing and aspiring teachers who seek to chart their own pathways and who are filled with compassion and high aspirations.

Johnson, L. (1992). *Dangerous minds*. New York, NY: St. Martin's Press.

Watch the movie, but do not forget to read the book. *Dangerous Minds* is the personal narrative of LouAnne Johnson's experience working in an urban school beset with all the "problems" that one often associates with "problem" students. Yet, the real story is not an apology or an exposé of the problems that seem to plague urban schooling. Nor is the story about demonizing the kids in the school. Rather, Johnson shows how teaching based on student needs and an understanding of their personal backgrounds can be transformative in the lives of students. All preconceived notions of teaching are up for grabs in this story.

Joseph, P. B., & Burnaford, G. E. (Eds.). (2001). *Images of schoolteachers in America* (2nd ed.). Mahwah, NJ: Lawrence Erlbaum.

This edited book contains 13 essays that explore images of schoolteachers in America from the beginning of the 20th century to the present. Relying upon various genres such as oral history, narrative, literature, popular culture, TV and film, the essays cover a wide gamut of issues including race, social class, gender, and authority. By focusing on both the social context and the actual experiences of teachers, the editors offer multidimensional and complex images of what it means to be a teacher. Among some of the arresting images portrayed within the book are progressive activist teachers and a retrospective on the cartoon show, *The Simpsons*. Collectively, *Images* invites experienced and aspiring teachers to think seriously about what has influenced and sustained our beliefs about teachers.

Kidder, T. (1990). *Among schoolchildren*. New York, NY: Harper Perennial.

"Mrs. Zajac wasn't born yesterday. She knows you didn't do your best work on this paper, Clarence. Don't you remember Mrs. Zajac saying that if you didn't do your best, she'd make you do it over again." With this opening Tracy Kidder takes you into the world of Christine Zajac, a fifth grade teacher in a racially mixed and poor school district in Holyoke, Massachusetts. Through the telling of the daily life of a teacher, Kidder helps his readers come to understand the frustrations and joys of teaching. In Kidder's account we also learn about the challenges a teacher faces as she tries to help all of her students learn, how teachers and administrators deal with each other, how parents and teachers interact, and even how to stock the classroom with Kleenex. Self-aware, full of ideas, disciplined, tough, and "with it" enough to know that she might be boring the kids, Mrs. Zajac is a teacher that each of us could learn from.

Miller, P. C. (Ed.). (2004). *Narratives from the classroom: An introduction to teaching.* **Thousand Oaks, CA: Sage Publications.**

Written by teachers and teacher educators, this book provides personal accounts of many important issues surrounding the purposes of education, the different policies and programs that influence the field of education, and the various practices found within different classrooms. Designed primarily for preservice students and anyone aspiring to be a teacher, *Narratives* encourages readers to analyze, reflect, and form their own conclusions about the issues presented. Of special interest to the preservice teacher is the chapter devoted to preparing for the job market told by a veteran school administrator.

two
Learning to Teach

From Student to Teacher

Who dares to teach must never cease to learn.

John Cotton Dana, 1912

Every job is a self-portrait of the person who did it. Autograph your work with excellence.

Unknown

FOCUS

In Chapter 1 you looked at your personal educational and musical history. There you began the process of identifying and articulating various influences on your beliefs and ideas about teaching. The organizing theme in Chapter 2 is learning to teach. A central idea in learning to teach is change and development with the belief that developmental growth is predicated on examining current teaching/learning experiences in light of future action. A significant goal of this chapter is coming to realize that change is a necessary part of development. Key questions explored in this chapter focus on how teachers become successful at what they do, how teachers learn to "act" like teachers, and how teachers begin to "think" like teachers.

Getting Started

How do teachers become successful at what they do, how do teachers learn to "act" like teachers, and how do teachers begin to "think" like teachers? To get started, however, we begin by interviewing teachers. What is it that experienced teachers know? What things influence their thinking? How is it that they decide to do one thing and not another?

Ask a Teacher

At one time or another a more experienced or practicing teacher you know has been where you are now—in a teacher education program learning about teaching. Practicing teachers—whether they are teaching high school choir, kindergarten, eighth grade geology, or are retired—are a wealth of information, and can be an important part in developing your understanding of the teaching profession. They too have musical proclivities, biographies, and historical journeys to share. Actually, as music educator and administrator Jeffrey Kimpton (2005) notes, the music education profession is like a huge ecosystem. There is a delicate balance between recruiting, preparing, and retaining teachers in the music education profession. Both the system and its balance rest on making connections with other people within the profession. As a member of the new generation of music teachers, it is always essential to connect with those in the field and to those who have gone before. One way to begin making connections and to start building a supporting and supportive network is by conducting interviews with music teachers. Interviews when they are focused on uncovering specific kinds of information can be powerful sources of knowledge. If you interview a teacher, she will probably tell you much about the life of teaching, including the emotional aspects of teaching that are often left out of the traditional course work found in preparation programs. There is much to learn from people who daily bridge the world of theory and the world of practice. Take a look at the photograph of this first year music teacher found in Figure 2.1. What questions might you ask her? What might you want to know about her, her students, the classroom, or the school? Examine Table 2.1 for some ideas for generating interview questions that come from traditional interviewing practices in qualitative research (Patton, 1990).

Interviews as a Source of Knowledge

At the root of any interview is dialogue—a conversation between two people. Although daily conversations are mostly informal and casual, think for a moment about the range of information, opinions, and ideas that are exchanged when engaged in a conversation with another person. What distinguishes interviews from conversations, however, is their explicit purpose and intent. Interviews are

FIGURE 2.1. First Year Music Teacher

TABLE 2.1 Ideas for Generating Interview Questions

Categories	Examples
Behaviors Questions about what a person has done or is doing.	*How do you choose the music you use in class? Do you choose different music depending upon the class you are teaching?* *What specific actions do you take to get a class started?*
Opinions/Values Questions about what a person thinks about a topic.	*What are the most important attributes you believe will lead to successful teaching? Why do you believe this?* *Often people think that teachers have a "cookbook of tricks" they use. What do think about this idea?*
Feelings Note that respondents sometimes respond with "I think . . ." so be careful to note that you are looking for feelings.	*Have there ever been times in your teaching where things seemed a bit too overwhelming?* *What does it feel like when you think you have done a wonderful job at teaching, and the students don't even seem to respond? What do you do then?*

Knowledge Questions designed to get facts or ideas about a topic.	*What learning theories have you found to be most helpful in your teaching?* *What ideas or theories have you come across that have helped you understand how to motivate learners?*
Sensory Questions about what people have seen, touched, heard, tasted or smelled. Consider musical experience here as well.	*What makes music a memorable musical experience?* *How do you help your orchestra students "feel" the rhythm of a piece?*
Background/Demographics Questions that include things such as education, experiences, etc.	*How long have you been teaching? How many degrees do you have? Have you always taught at the same school, level?*

designed to gain specific information and/or thoughts, and are almost always goal driven. Although there are many reasons for conducting interviews, one goal that preservice music teachers might pursue is that of building a more sophisticated understanding of the complexities and particularities of a music teacher's experience. Another goal may be to "see into" or connect to the lives of children you may be teaching through the thinking of a practicing teacher.

As you get ready to interview take a few moments to reflect on what you wrote in TAKE ACTION 1.4 (Successful Teacher/Unsuccessful Teacher) in Chapter 1. Recall specifically that in writing your profile on the Unsuccessful Teacher, we noted that there was no need to identify an individual by name. There was an important reason for this, and that has to do with ethics, and the way we portray individuals. In general, ethics deal with certain codes of conduct that you should use to guide your actions and judgments of others. Certainly, respect for one's self, others, and your surroundings is an important code by which to live. As a member of a profession, there are certain standards that you should use. Three that are often cited in teaching are: fairness, duty to the profession, and responsibility to the general public. As you prepare for and engage in this exercise, keep the idea of ethics in the forefront of your mind. Also take a look at Appendix 1: Ethics of Going Into The Field.

Learning to Teach and Teacher Development

The answers to what experienced teachers know, the things that influence their thinking, and how they decide to do one thing and not another are as varied as the

TAKE ACTION 2.1
Gaining Insight from Interviewing Teachers in the Field

This Take Action is designed to gain greater insight into the teaching life by conducting interviews with practicing teachers.

Getting Started with the Interview

- Identify a teacher to interview.
- Prepare for the interview by writing questions (See Table 2.1 for ideas on generating interview questions).

Setting up the Interview

- Contact the teacher you want to interview in advance.
- Choose a setting with as little distraction as possible. Arrange a specific time and place. Indicate approximately how much time the interview will require. Check to see if there are any security clearances that you need to know about if you are going to meet at a school.
- Offer your teacher an outline of topics to be covered. Ask if he or she has any questions before you meet.
- If you want to electronically record the interview, ask and get permission.

Preparing for the Interview

- Prepare an "information sheet" that includes what you already know about the teacher. Also make sure to document day, time spent, place.
- Decide on and write out the goals for the interview.
- Write out a list of questions in advance.
- Decide what questions are of highest priority.
- Allow for questioning opportunities that may emerge out of your talk with the teacher.
- Obtain and test your equipment and batteries, if you are recording the interview.

Meeting the Teacher

- Dress like a future member of the music teaching profession.
- Bring a notebook and writing instruments, along with your prepared questions.
- Keep notes, jot down important things said.
- If you electronically record the interview, make sure you ask first. (See Setting up the Interview.)
- Make eye contact with the teacher as much as possible, even while you are jotting down notes.

- Try to stick to the questions prepared, but be flexible enough to "go with the flow." Your teacher may provide some valuable information about topics that you never considered. Be alert, and capture the information.

After the Interview

- Send a thank you note, and remember to say thank you at the end of the interview.
- Go over your notes immediately making elaborations on jottings; where you see holes, fill in with reminders; make clarifications.
- Create a report as soon as possible after the interview. Memories work best when they are the freshest in our minds.
- Send a copy of the report to the teacher you interview. Ask the teacher to read your report and confirm that it is an accurate representation of the ideas expressed. This is not only an act of courtesy but also an important part of a professional interview. If you need to make revisions, do so, and then ask your interviewee to verify them. Repeat this process until both of you feel comfortable about what is to be presented.

Presenting What You Have Learned

Go over your report and prepare a brief description of the teacher or teachers you interviewed. Compare and discuss your reports with a classmate or get together with a small group from class. Are there any commonalities across each person's interview report? What seems distinctive? Try constructing category themes using the group's set of interviews. Look for common characteristics that might be organized into groups or categories of ideas. For example, each interview report might mention an important event that in some way influenced or shaped a teacher's viewpoint, belief, or practice. Share your analysis with others.

TAKE ACTION 2.2
Examining the Professional Development of Your College Professors

The purpose of this Take Action is to think about the professional development of your college professors and to discover the major influences that acted as catalysts in the development of their careers.

There are several ways to carry out this inquiry. One way is for you to make an appointment to interview one of your professors. This might not be possible if you are in a large class. However, if you are a member of a class, you may want to divide into partners or teams to complete this exercise. Another option might be to invite the faculty to serve on a panel and then have a class member serve as moderator. Electronic chats may also be an option.

In any case, before you meet with any of the faculty, spend some time generating sets of questions aimed at ascertaining important events or influences in their careers. Listed below are some categories to help you create your questions. Feel free to generate more.

- Major influences on their thinking
- Major people in their professional lives
- Places taught or positions held
- Colleges and universities attended
- Important musical, personal, professional (and other) experiences
- Skills acquired
- Moments of change or rethinking related to learning and teaching
- Beliefs sustained or maintained over time, beliefs jettisoned or disposed of
- Struggles or frustrations encountered and overcome
- Personally rewarding events or situations
- Challenges embraced.

After the Interview

Prepare a brief report on what you find or what was revealed at the panel session. Your report will be dependent upon how you organized the interviews. Consider some of the following options. Feel free to come up with additional ideas.

- Compare your report with a classmate or get together with a small group from class. Are there any commonalities across each faculty member's career path? What seems distinctive among each faculty member's interview?
- Try constructing a professional development profile for a specific faculty member or for the faculty as a whole. You can use your questions as a basis for developing your profile or you could look for common characteristics within each of the interviewee's responses that might be organized into a group or categories of ideas. For example, each interview might mention the importance of a particular teaching position held.

As a conclusion, discuss how change functioned as a transforming mechanism in professional growth and development. Or, discuss what important event, idea or skill helped most in their area of expertise or in their teaching.

teachers we talk to. A teacher's professional development is quite unique, often complex, and almost always dependent on specific decisions to be made in a particular context. However, if we were to look at an individual's teaching over his or her career, we might be able to discern several distinct phases of growth and change. Most often the life span of a teaching career is characterized as follows:

- Pre-collegiate (from birth to entering college)
- Preservice or collegiate years
- Induction years (first five to seven years of teaching)
- Professional years
- Professional maturity and winding down

Many researchers have looked at these individual phases of a teacher's professional development and have tried to describe the characteristics, concerns, and needs that emerge over time. Some researchers have focused on the preservice years—traditionally the college undergraduate years. Others have looked at what might be seen as overall development—from preservice to retirement. Still others have concentrated on just one or two phases of career development. The induction phase of teaching—the first five years or so—has recently become of interest, especially in terms of the kinds of mentoring strategies that help novice teachers adapt and thrive in their new teaching environments. Most theories and studies of teacher growth and development show that teachers have different sets of knowledges, skills, and dispositions at different points in their careers. They also have different needs and concerns. In a developmental conception of learning to teach, teaching is not necessarily something that is learned and then done over and over again. Rather, teaching is about always learning and being a "student of teaching." Of special interest to students in the preservice phase of teacher development is the research devoted to what has been called "concerns theory." At the heart of concerns theory is a focus on teacher thinking and actions.

Concerns Theory: An Enduring Description of Teacher Development

In the 1960s, Frances Fuller (1969) conducted an important and pioneering study that looked at teacher education students' concerns about teaching. After analyzing students' responses to open-ended statements and interviews, Fuller proposed three different phases of concerns related to teaching: *self, task, and impact*. Concerns related to self deal primarily with feelings of adequacy and competence, and focus on questions such as "How am I doing? Will my students like me?" Classroom discipline is a primary concern at this phase. Initially, Fuller called this the "survival" stage of development. Task concerns prompt questions that relate to assimilating pedagogical knowledge or focus on time and logistics of teaching. "What music should I choose?" "What is the best way to teach a specific concept?"

"Did I 'cover' my lesson plan?" Impact concerns represent a shift in focus to students and student learning. Concerns at this phase include topics such as motivation, individual differences in learners, and achievement and accomplishment of students. "Is everyone learning in this class?" "How can learners' feelings of accomplishment be increased?"

Fuller and Bown (1975) hypothesized that student teachers would naturally move through these concerns as they progressed through a teacher education program. Recent work in concerns theory suggests that this is an idealized model, and that the progression from self to task to impact concerns does not always occur. Borich (2000), for example, points out that a teacher's concerns may be more cyclical than linear. Experienced teachers may indeed be at phase three in their current context (concern for impact), but when placed in unfamiliar environments, revert to concerns that reflect earlier phases (concerns about self or task, for example). This understanding highlights the importance and potential power of context on a teacher's development and growth. Rather than progressing neatly through set stages of development, teachers' awareness and understanding of school and teaching environments, as well as their perceptions of themselves and their profession, must be taken into account when describing teachers' growth and development. As we have seen elsewhere, personal beliefs play a profound role in shaping your thoughts and dispositions about education and how effective you think you will be at teaching. Although not substantiated by any large body of research, your own sense of personal effectiveness may have an important bearing on whether you will choose to continue in the profession or leave it. In other words, your long-term involvement in teaching may be a reflection of your own ability to produce desired results (Huberman, 1992).

Teacher concerns have been extensively studied in general education, but less so among music teacher education students. Concerns theory, however, remains a robust idea in thinking about change and development. As a matter of fact, Fuller's approach has even been used to study the change process in general, with the idea that an individual's thoughts and feelings about change could be classified around types of concerns (Hall, Wallace & Dossett, 1973). Moreover, concerns theory has been used as a basis for planning continuing professional development activities in education, primarily due to its focus on the teacher and the need for generating new ways of dealing with issues.

TAKE ACTION 2.3
What Concerns Do You have about Music Teaching?

Think about an aspect related to teaching that you might have some concern over. If you are in a methods class, you may have some anxiety over a specific teaching task or the use of particular strategies. If you are currently working with students in a field experience, you might be feeling anxious over the kind of impact you might have. Or, you may be more concerned about what others are thinking of you or the image of teaching you want to project. For example, if you had to stand up in front of a middle school band tomorrow and lead the group, what might you be concerned about?

One way to address your concerns is to "map out the territory" and devise a "chart for self-guidance." Take a few moments to:

- Identify a specific teaching/learning context (methods class, field experience, practicum, etc.).
- Identify areas or topics within this context where you are feeling a bit anxious or feel that you need to know more about.
- Transform your feelings and thinking into concerns—that is, make explicit your worries. These should be of personal importance to your goal of learning to teach music.
- Transform your concerns into goals that contain action plans for addressing your concerns.

Articulating concerns and generating personal teaching goals helps provide you with a basis for achieving confidence and competence in your teaching. Concerns and goals also provide a basis for reflection on growth and your ability to feel self-empowered. Both self-efficacy and personal action rely on meeting your concerns head on and devising specific action plans to address them.

At Close Range 2.1 presents some examples of teaching concerns from music education students who have finished a methods course in general music. Each student is just getting ready to spend an entire semester twice a week working with elementary-age learners. This is their first "formal" teaching experience.

AT CLOSE RANGE 2.1
Into the Field—Concerns and Goals

Karla's Concern: *I have not had much experience working with students in the upper levels of elementary school. Since I am teaching fifth and sixth grade this semester, one of my concerns is not knowing enough about age-appropriate repertoire and activities. Personally, I do not remember much about sixth grade, except that I hated it. On the other hand, I loved fifth grade. I have spent so much time working with children from pre-K to third grade, I really want to get to know about fifth and sixth graders and what interests them.*

Goal: *Since I feel somewhat lost in finding activities and repertoire for fifth and sixth grade students, I will refer back to my general music methods materials and* *binder and see what resources and information I have there. I will also refer to the MENC handbook I received about strategies for teaching middle level general music. In order to find more information, I can use the resources in the School of Music's Materials and Curriculum Lab and University Library, as well as the knowledge of the faculty. With all of these resources readily available, in addition to getting into the classroom and seeing what the students are able to do, I hope to develop a greater knowledge of teaching fifth and sixth grade general music.*

Laura's Concern: *Because we are being teamed and will have to work together as a group, I am apprehensive about working as a cohesive group of teachers.*

Goal: *I realize that I am a person who doesn't work well in groups and I hope to step beyond that in this collaborative teaching effort. Our first few sessions have somewhat quelled my reticence and made me realize that I am working with two capable musicians. I aspire to make sure that I don't "bite off more than I can chew" and look to spread the burdens of teaching amongst the three of us. In addition, I aim to make planning periods as useful as possible while building team cohesion. I believe that if we all pull our share of the work, all should work out for the best.*

What do Karla's and Laura's concerns and goals reveal about their anxieties related to their impending teaching experience? At first glance, Karla seems to be apprehensive about her ability to attend to the "tasks of teaching." Clearly she is worried about selecting materials that she believes should be interesting for fifth and sixth graders. A closer reading of Karla's concerns, however, suggests that she may be more concerned about her own well-being in working with sixth graders, than anything else. The search for appropriate materials and content actually serves as a vehicle through which her self concern emerges. Self concerns are rarely just about oneself. They are usually in relation to the learners we are teaching, to subject matter issues, to the environment we find ourselves in or to others who might have an influence on our teaching. Fundamentally Karla's concern and goal focus on her ability to prepare age-appropriate lessons. Karla's goal is important because it specifically identifies an action plan that addresses her needs. Her goal is also powerful in that it acts as a compass point in orienting her actions. Often the articulation of goals reveals more about our focus of concern than the actual articulation of the concern itself. Laura, on the other hand, is clearly focused on her self. Both the tasks of teaching and the impact that her teaching (and her team's teaching) may have on learners' potentials are nowhere to be found in her concern or her goal. Laura is seeking and planning a way to survive her initial entry into the classroom.

We invite you to read a short excerpt from a research study exploring an undergraduate's experiences in learning to teach music (Campbell, 1999). This excerpt is taken from a more extended narrative written by a third year music education student and the researcher. As you read Emily's story, keep in mind that this was her first "formal" teaching experience. Although she had many informal teaching experiences, her placement in a first grade general music class, under the mentorship of a university faculty member, raised a number of concerns. The excerpt also highlights other issues associated with personal beliefs, and constructing a teacher identity.

AT CLOSE RANGE 2.2
Emily's First Months of Teaching: Twirling in Circles

Facing a group of 25 first graders was not an overwhelming fear of Emily's, but thinking up strategies for keeping them engaged in activities, and for moving them from one place in the room to another as "quickly and quietly" as possible was. Emily's sense of not being able to "control" or manage the class became a significant issue that she sought consciously to address. Getting "control" over the students' behavior and focusing their attention on the lesson became a priority of Emily's early in the practicum. Emily's plan to get control of managing the class was also the beginning of a personal negotiating process for her—one that meant reconstructing her "friend" image of teaching into a different teacher image—one focused on something she later called a more "realistic" idea of teaching.

Emily's initial attempts "to get the class to run smoothly" were focused on designing lessons that had lots of materials and different activities. She dropped songs that "did not work," because students were just "not interested," and she also tried to "overplan," thinking that if she had too much to do, then she would not have any behavior problems. But Emily still found it difficult to respond to situations where children were talking while she was talking, or "twirling in circles on the floor" after she asked them to stop, or running away from the class circle during lesson transitions, in a way in which she felt she had no control. At one point, Emily said, "I just don't know what to do."

Emily was rather critical about, or "edgy" as she said, having to "correct" students' behavior for fear of quelling their interests and for fear of not being perceived as a "friendly teacher." Emily consciously tried to talk to the class in a "pleasant, quiet gentle tone," and did not want to raise her voice for fear of it sounding like yelling. "Yelling at a child was not what a teacher should do." But, one day Emily did decide to raise her voice when the class was "particularly wired" and "got the response" she wanted, that is, the class stopped talking and listened to her. Afterwards she said:

> *I was able to finish the lesson, and learning took place. I don't think they hated me, they didn't test me any longer, and I think perhaps I gained some respect because I had shown some authority that hadn't been displayed before.* (Campbell, 1999, p. 24–25)

What does the excerpt from Emily's narrative tell us about her experience of learning to teach music? Like Karla's and Laura's concerns, we can apply Fuller's theory to Emily's story. In this analysis we might able to say that many of Emily's concerns were self and survival related. For example, Emily felt a need to be liked and a need for respect. She desired having some kind of personal control over managing the classroom. She had a vague sense that her lesson planning was not quite right, and felt a need to appear to be competent in what she was doing. If we were to re-read Emily's story and look for task and impact-related concerns, we would be hard pressed to find any. Like many novice teachers, when they are placed in "real-live" teaching contexts, the immediate exigencies or demands of the classroom seem overwhelming. According to one theory of teacher development, until novice teachers can "get a handle" on classroom rules, rituals, and routines, little development in professional growth is likely to occur (Furlong & Maynard, 1995).

All music teachers must acquire certain types of knowledge, skills, and dispositions to be effective teachers. It is important for prospective teachers to ask and be aware of what types of knowledge and experiences will aid them in the profession, as well as determine how to address them in their development as music teachers. If Fuller's theory is correct, then your first teaching concern is likely to be for your own well-being. Certainly, this seems to be the case in the three student narratives we have examined. Your *self* concerns should be followed by a greater attention to teaching skills and mastery of content, then by a focus on student learning. But is this always so? Read the Focus on Research 2.1 describing Preservice Music Teachers' Concerns about Teaching. After you finish reading the summary and the implications provided, do your own speculating as to why preservice music teachers' concerns seem to follow the path the researchers found.

FOCUS ON RESEARCH 2.1
Preservice Music Teachers' Concerns about Teaching

Mark Robin Campbell and Linda K. Thompson (2007) were interested in studying the concerns of preservice music education teachers across four different points in professional development. From 16 institutions of higher education in the United States, 1121 preservice music education teachers participated in the study. Each participant was asked to indicate:

- The class in which they were currently enrolled (Introduction to Music Education, Methods Class, Field Experience–Practicum [minimum of 50% of class time site-based], or Student Teaching). These classes were used as indicators of increasing levels of teacher development and served as a cross sample for teacher development.
- A single primary teaching interest (choir, band, orchestra, general music, or other), and
- A single desired teaching level (early childhood, elementary, middle school/junior high school, high school, or college/university).

To measure students' concerns, Campbell and Thompson used the Teacher

Concerns Checklist (Borich, 2000)—a 45 item survey that contained statements related to self, task or impact concerns. The survey was based upon Fuller and Bown's (1975) three-stage model of teacher development.

Analysis of the data indicated that:

- Field Experience students held higher levels of concerns than did students in Introduction to Music Education, Methods, and Student Teaching.
- Females, regardless of teaching interest or desired teaching level, showed higher concerns than males.
- Participants indicating a preference to teach elementary level or university level showed higher concerns than those intending to teach high school.
- Regardless of teaching interest or desired teaching level, impact concerns ranked highest, followed by self concerns, with task concerns ranked lowest. Findings suggested a departure from the sequence of Fuller and Bown's (1975) concerns theory.

Several interpretations and implications can be drawn from these findings:

- Consistent with other findings about teachers' concerns, this study supports the premise that preservice and novice teachers hold varying levels of concerns *simultaneously* (Guillaume & Rudney, 1993).
- Preservice teachers may be moving through teacher education programs with "unrealistic optimism" about their teaching skills and abilities because the scores for all three areas of concern seemed to hover around the "moderately concerned" level rather than "highly concerned."
- The low position of task scores (among all participants) may be related to the idea that preservice teachers may lack the kinds of pedagogical content knowledge and skills required to engage students in music in a meaningful way. There may even be a "disconnect" between preservice teachers' concerns for the tasks of teaching and having the skills necessary to effectively make an impact.
- Because field experience/practicum students held higher levels of concern, the idea that levels of concern are highly contextual bears further investigation.
- The high position of impact scores indicates a clear desire among preservice music teachers to create a lasting impact on their students.

Campbell and Thompson recommended that students at all levels within the music teacher education program be placed in "real live" teaching contexts, because it is here that concern levels are likely to be elevated. Moreover, it is in having the responsibility of teaching that a greater "need to know" arises on the part of the preservice teachers.

TAKE ACTION 2.4
Interviewing Student Teachers

This Take Action is designed to ascertain "insider" knowledge about the concerns of student teachers. Find a student teacher and conduct an interview based upon the ideas discussed in Fuller's concerns theory. If you are currently student teaching, find another student teacher to interview.

While asking specific questions related to each of the concerns, consider asking questions that relate to how the student teacher's concerns emerged or changed over time; for example, was there a linear progression that moved from self, to task to impact or did concerns appear to emerge "randomly," dependent upon context—event or circumstance, interaction with student or another teacher or materials? Table 2.2 shows how you might organize questions around each concern: self, task and impact.

TABLE 2.2 Concerns and Questions Derived from Fuller's Theory

Concern	Description and Focus	Potential Questions
Self	Deals primarily with feelings of adequacy and competence, and focuses on questions such as "How am I doing? Will my students like me?"	*When you think about respect, what concerns you most about teaching?* *When you think about being observed, what worries you?*
Task	Relates to assimilating pedagogical knowledge or focuses on time and logistics of teaching. "What music should I choose?" "What is the best way to teach a specific concept?"	*When you think about designing a lesson based upon a specific concept, what concerns you most about it?* *What standards (or musical activities) concern you most when it comes to teaching or planning a lesson?*
Impact	Represents a shift in focus to students and student learning. Concerns at this phase include areas such as motivation, individual differences in learners, and achievement and accomplishment of students. "Is everyone learning in this class?"	*When you think about helping your students value musical learning, what concerns you most?* *What concerns do you have in regard to increasing students' feelings of accomplishment?*

After the Interview

Prepare a brief report on what you find and share with a classmate or in class. In preparing your report, you may want to consider the extent to which the individual you interviewed falls predominately within one or another of the concern stages. Consider also whether or not he or she tended to progress through the stages in a linear fashion or a non-linear fashion. Try to figure out if any event or set of circumstances had any bearing on moving from one constellation of concerns to another.

Growth and Development of Professional Knowledge: From Student to Novice Teacher

Nearly two and one-half decades after Fuller offered the concerns theory of teacher development, Furlong and Maynard (1995) took another look at professional development using a similar perspective. They found comparable results and noted professional growth to be predicated on shifts related to concerns, as well as teachers' growth in confidence and competence. Interestingly though, Furlong and Maynard observed that growth was dependent upon reflection on practice, and that the nature and content of reflection differed according to the stage student teachers were in. The strength of their research is that much of it is empirically derived. That is, Furlong and Maynard worked with student teachers while they were student teaching, and as a result of their work created practical applications from what they found.

In brief, Furlong and Maynard's research shows a developmental path that moves from "practical" to more "global" concerns and progresses through four distinct stages. The general progression, however, is similar to Fuller's; that is, there is a movement from self concerns to task concerns to impact concerns. In the first stage, student teachers often held and displayed idealistic views about teaching and their own roles as a teacher. They wanted to be liked by their students and sought to develop caring, warm, and nurturing environments. (Recall Emily's story—her initial image of teaching was that of "being a friend.") The student teachers were influenced by and often modeled themselves after significant teachers from their own school experiences, without considering implications of their own practice. (Here you might recall, from Chapter 1, influences on college students' decisions to become music teachers.) After initial experiences in the classroom, teachers' concerns shifted away from their early ideals to more immediate concerns of survival, classroom control, and the desire to fit into their immediate working environment. The focus of their own growth related primarily to management skills and how others perceived them. (Here again, we can think of Emily's story and how "twirling in circles" acted as a catalyst in changing her thinking and actions.) Movement into stage three was characterized by the extent to which teachers were able to establish a sense of authority as a teacher and develop workable teaching strategies. In many cases, students would often adopt the teaching styles and characteristics of the host or cooperating teachers. More generally, growth was seen as a shift away from self concerns toward a greater focus on students as learners. In the fourth stage, some student teachers reached a plateau. Concerns of control were refocused on student learning. To move beyond the plateau, student teachers needed prompting to get them to think about a deeper understanding of teaching.

In addition to providing insight into the development of student teachers, the importance of Furlong and Maynard's work can be seen in how different learning goals for student teachers' growth can be articulated if movement to the next stage of development is to occur. Also powerful in Furlong and Maynard's model are the strategies they offer for mentors and various roles that best facilitate student teacher growth. Table 2.3 shows their model of student teacher development and appropriate mentoring strategies. Another interesting question, suggested by one of our preservice teachers after studying Furlong and Maynard's stages of development, centers on the extent to which the developmental stages are natural. That is, are all preservice teachers likely to follow the same path in the same order? That model would assume so, but with mentoring and with student teachers' "eyes" looking at the "big developmental picture," perhaps some phases might be combined. From a teacher education perspective, more integration leading to more sophisticated understandings of teaching along with a more concentrated focus on learners is desirable.

TABLE 2.3 Mentoring Student Teacher Development

Phases	Student Teacher Learning Focus	Mentoring Role and Strategies
Beginning Teaching	Classroom rules, rituals and routines	Role = Model
	Establishing authority or a "teaching presence"	Help student teachers learn how to observe experienced teachers
		Collaborative teaching focused on skills used to create rules and routines
Supervised Teaching	Teaching/Instruction Competencies	Role = Coach
		Observe and provide specific feedback on instruction
		Facilitate reflection-on-action

From Teaching to Learning	Understanding pupil learning	<u>Role = Critical Friend</u>
	Developing effective teaching	Challenge beliefs to help see the complexities of teaching
	Transition from "acting like a teacher" to "thinking like a teacher"	Observe and re-examine lesson planning in relation to pupil learning, subject matter understanding
Autonomous Teaching	Investigating the grounds for practice	<u>Role = Co-Inquirer</u>
		Help broaden repertoire of strategies to deepen understanding of complexities, including social, moral and political dimensions
		Partnership teaching— joint planning, teaching and debriefing

Note: Compiled and adapted from J. Furlong & T. Maynard (1995). *Mentoring student teachers: The growth of professional knowledge* (pp. 178–195). London and New York: Routledge.

TAKE ACTION 2.5
Conferencing with Cooperating Teachers

Meet with your school's Collegiate MENC Chapter and plan a mini-conference devoted to mentoring during the student teaching experience. Invite practicing music teachers who often serve as cooperating or sponsor teachers for music education student teachers to serve on a panel. For topic discussion, prepare a list of questions for each of the phases of development as identified by Furlong and Maynard. Base your questions on *student teacher learning goals*. Elect a moderator or ask your Chapter Advisor to serve as moderator. Some questions to consider asking:

- As a cooperating teacher, what strategies do you use to help a student teacher acquire specific classroom management routines? (Phase 1—Beginning Teaching)
- In your experience what does "acting like a teacher" mean? What does "thinking like a teacher" mean? How do you see the two related? (Phase 3—Teaching to Learning)

- How do you help student teachers "match learning activities" with students' needs and interests, and how do you help student teachers ascertain how students learn best? (Phase 3—Teaching to Learning)
- What are some ways you use to challenge student teachers' beliefs about teaching? (Phase 3—Teaching to Learning)
- How do you help student teachers learn how to observe another teacher? What are some specific things to look for? (Phase 1—Beginning Teaching)
- What is the best way to help a student teacher learn to see beyond his or her own "horizons?" In other words, how do you prompt a student teacher to consider new ways of looking at things? (Phase 4—Autonomous Teaching)
- When you work with student teachers on planning, how do you encourage them to focus on student learning, as compared to demonstrating a specific teaching technique? In other words, how do you help student teachers look at the content of their lessons, rather than their own "performances" of lessons? (Phase 2—Supervised Teaching)
- What do you see as the teacher's role in facilitating student learning? (Phase 3—Teaching to Learning)

Note: There are several ways to carry out this panel conference. If resources and equipment permit try using interactive videoconferencing.

The organizing theme for this chapter has been learning to teach. Clearly learning to teach as a topic is much more complex than what we were able to explore here. Likewise, we were only able to scratch the surface on understanding how teachers become successful at what they do, how they learn to "act" like teachers, and how they begin to "think" like teachers. These are equally complex ideas. Throughout the chapter, however, we have encouraged you to think about these ideas and more generally the notion of learning to teach as a matter of change and development. We have also asked you to begin to articulate your current thinking in light of immediate and future action. We have asked you to seek out the thinking of others and begin to use their experiences as a springboard for your own growth and development. As you continue to seek understanding of yourself, the tasks of teaching, and the impact you have, we encourage you to learn to make connections with people in the field and with those who have gone before. Building a network of supporting colleagues at various places in their own development will help propel you forward in your own growth and development from student to teacher.

For Your Inquiry

Burke, J., and Krajicek, J. (2006). *Letters to a new teacher: A month-by-month guide to the year ahead.* **Portsmouth, NH: Heinemann.**

Written to allay the fears and concerns of a first year teacher, *Letters to a New Teacher* addresses a whole gamut of topics, including classroom management, creating teaching units, boundaries of student–teacher relationships, student suicide and sexual abuse, teacher self-doubt, "testing season" to name a few. Although Jim Burke speaks from his position as an English teacher, his ideas are useful, humorous and practical. A better mentor—one who is supportive, experienced and reliable—regardless of subject matter specialty—could not be found. Inspirational, poetic and honest.

Kane, P. R. (Ed.). (1996). *My first year as a teacher.* **New York, NY: Signet.**

Edited by Pearl Rock Kane, 25 first-year teachers "tell tales" from their first year of teaching. Included are stories of frustrations, joy, memorable students, and resentful colleagues. Not left out in these tales are schools that represent a cross sampling of classrooms in America—the handicapped, the disadvantaged and the privileged. In the final analysis, each story reminds the reader of the importance of teaching and the joys to be found.

Wong, H. K., & Wong, R. T. (1998). *The first days of school: How to be an effective teacher.* **Mountain View, CA: Harry K. Wong.**

With over several million copies sold, *The First Days of School* has to be one of the all-time reads for teachers. Regardless of your stage of professional development or where you are in your career, this book has tips on just about anything related to teaching. Included are chapters devoted to classroom management, teaching for mastery, creating positive expectations, and professional growth.

three
Learning from Others

Understanding Teacher Career Development

What most fundamentally characterizes the well adjusted, or highly sane person is not chiefly the particular habits or attitudes that he holds, but rather the deftness with which he modifies them in response to changing circumstances.

Wendell Johnson

FOCUS

In this chapter we invite you to "learn from others," and become more familiar with teaching as a lifelong career. We have several aims: first, to engage you in the process of looking beyond your immediate concerns and goals of learning to teach music and peek into the future; and second, to expand your field of vision by considering the various influences, factors, knowledges, skills, competencies, and dispositions that can shape a life in teaching over time. A key concept in this chapter is coming to understand that the general progression of one's career is not just shaped by the conditions and environments in which we find ourselves. Rather, we can act as agents in shaping conditions and contexts. In other words, we can be the "authors" of own careers.

Getting Started

It may seem unusual to think about "lifelong career development" as a music teacher if you are currently an undergraduate student in a preparation or certification program. Retiring from a "long and distinguished" career in music education probably isn't where your main interests or concerns are right now. If you are like many undergraduate music education majors, your immediate concern is probably with whether or not your technical and expressive skills on your instrument will garner your first chair in an ensemble or whether you will pass the end of semester jury with high praise. Thinking about and analyzing the social conditions that contribute to impoverished professional working environments may be literally and figuratively "out of sight." Wondering about teaching routines and how they may lead to boredom or "teacher burnout" may even seem odd or even discouraging, especially when initial concerns during the first years of teaching may be more about acquiring routines rather than changing them. Looking at teaching over the long haul, including the concerns and issues that accompany lifelong learning, however, is essential if teachers are to become dynamic members of the music teaching profession.

Although empirical evidence of the challenges music teachers face in their daily lives is scant, our personal observations and conversations with other teachers in the music profession tell us that teaching is not easy. We know that nearly one-half of all newly hired teachers leave the profession within the first five years (US Department of Education: National Center for Education Statistics, 2005). In a recent symposium on music teacher education, Ingersoll (2001) noted that teachers leave their careers due to three reasons:

1. lack of support (primarily administrative, from other areas as well),
2. lack of influence (in decision making processes, curriculum work), and
3. inadequate professional development activities (including early and continuous mentoring).

The actual rate of attrition and the specific factors for why music teachers leave the profession is unknown. Music teacher educators, however, have not ignored the concerns Ingersoll's research has uncovered. Manny Brand (2002), for example, suggests that one of the best services the profession might provide to prospective teachers is to have serious and deep conversations about professional life issues: "issues that are personally relevant and intellectually meaningful . . ." Table 3.1 shows some of Brand's questions for thinking about deeper issues associated with music teaching. We encourage you to think about these questions and begin a conversation with your current classmates and former music teachers. We also encourage you to think seriously about the difficulties that a career in teaching music may have in store.

As we begin a more focused look into teachers' career growth and development, two observations to keep in mind might be useful. First, a closer look at the lives of

TABLE 3.1 Developing a Deeper Understanding of Music Teaching

Questions

- *What does it mean to be a music teacher?*

- *How do music teachers reconcile the dignity and beauty of music with the ugliness of school violence?*

- *What are the dreams, hopes, and fears of music teachers?*

- *How do music teachers maintain their sense of calling and altruism when faced with disillusionment in music teaching?*

- *Why do teachers receive so little professional status in their schools and within American society?*

- *How do music teachers reconcile their original idealized images of "saving" students from a troubled youth, negligent family, or poor environment with their actual experiences?*

- *Are music teachers valued and are their contributions recognized in their communities?*

teachers can help you build a more realistic conception of teaching as a career. As Manny Brand notes, "music education does not need overly enthusiastic proselytizers to portray music teaching simplistically and unrealistically—as an easy career and a perfect or trouble-free path to job satisfaction based simply on a love of music" (2002, p. 46). Examining the typical struggles and achievements of teachers can lay a foundation for recognizing in our own personal teaching when we might need to adjust thinking, try out new practices or seek help from others. Second, studying the "complex responsibilities, intensity and range of demands, fatigue, multiple tasks, and sophisticated music, educational, and personal skills require[d] of music teachers" (Brand, 2002, p. 44) can help you build a more sophisticated understanding of the challenges teachers face in pursuing a life in teaching. Exploring the "walk" and "talk" of a career helps us understand better the connection between why we chose music teaching in the first place and the difficulties and joys we may encounter as we mature in the profession. We know that dedication and commitment counts; both figure prominently in achievement and getting things done. But according to Brand and others in the profession, it still has to be more than "love of music" and "love of kids."

Teachers' Career Growth and Development: Cycles and Stages

Take a look at Table 3.2 "Four Theories of Professional Development in a Teaching Career." The first column in the Table shows five major phases in many teachers' careers: pre-collegiate, preservice, induction, professional, and finally the career "wind down." The header row identifies four prominent theories that describe how

TABLE 3.2 Four Theories of Professional Development in a Teaching Career

Phase	Theory			
	"Four Stages of Teachers' Growth" Frede	"The Teacher Career Cycle" Fessler	"The Lives of Teachers" Huberman	"Exemplary Teaching" Berliner
Pre-Collegiate	---------Pre-K through High School---------			
Preservice	---------College Teacher Education Program---------			
Induction	Mastering the Nuts and Bolts	Induction	Exploration and Stabilization	Novice
	Too Much of a Good Thing			Advanced Beginner
	Do it My Way			
Professional	Creative Adaptation	Competency Building		Competent Teacher
		Enthusiastic and Growing	Experimentation/ Activism	
		Career Frustration		Proficient Teacher
		Stability	Conservatism or Regret	Expert
Career Wind Down		Career Wind-Down		
		Career Exit		

teachers develop within their careers. What do these theories have in common? How are they different? What might you learn from these theories for your own professional development? Like many other areas within music teacher education, there is no specific theory or description of the growth and development processes devoted to music teachers and their careers. However, we believe that there is likely to be significant overlap between the career paths of music teachers and teachers in general.

How Teachers Grow: A Closer Look at Teacher Learning

How do beginning teachers learn to teach? When confronted with new teaching situations and curricular challenges, Ellen Frede (2003) suggests that teachers' understanding of learning to teach can be seen as a four-stage process. Frede's analysis is based upon reflecting on her own growth as a teacher and her work as a mentor to beginning teachers. Frede's four stages are: (a) "Mastering the Nuts and Bolts," (b) "Too Much of a Good Thing," (c) "Do it My Way," and (d) "Creative Adaptation."

Mastering the Nuts and Bolts. At the heart of mastering the nuts and bolts of teaching is gaining control over structural and curricular elements that create classroom environments for learning. The day-to-day running of a classroom, along with effective ways to guide learning is of central concern. Central to creating productive learning environments is mastering the details of curricular planning—clearly thinking about and communicating *how* an activity should be carried out, including *for whom* the activity is intended and *for what* purposes. Although interested in developing a deeper understanding of curricular aims and practices, beginning teachers often have difficulty seeing the "big picture," or understanding the rationales behind the specific elements of lessons they teach. A key question to promote professional growth is: To what extent have I built in time in my daily activities for reflecting on my planning and teaching? Making time for reflection is not only necessary for thinking about the effectiveness of your work, but also for the philosophical reasons that undergird all teacher planning and actions.

Too Much of a Good Thing. At this second phase, teachers are comfortable with the structural elements of classrooms and start to hone in on their own teaching styles. According to Frede, teachers "tend to practice one new strategy for a period of time until it is a natural part of their interactions with children. The limitation is that they often use this strategy to the exclusion of others" (2003, p. 21). For example, someone might describe your teaching as akin to that of a "manager"—one who wants students to solve problems independently and within groups, but who is also constantly concerned about maintaining an orderly classroom. Or, someone might describe you as a "free-wheeler"—one who allows students a great deal of free choice, but forgets to set limits that would create a safe, secure learning environment. In both cases, the concern is that you might be using a single strategy to the exclusion of other methods that might be more effective or appropriate.

Although mastery of a specific teaching strategy is important, it may, however, be too much of good thing. For example, *consistency* may be key in classroom management, but *variety* may be necessary for motivation. Key questions that address career development at this stage include: To what extent do my teaching practices exhibit diversity in range and scope? To what extent do I seek ideas from others about alternative strategies for addressing student learning needs? As in learning how to develop classroom structures, reflection on how you spend your time in the classroom and what did and did not work for learners is helpful in avoiding a "one size fits all" approach.

Do it My Way. Teachers at this third phase of development usually possess an excellent understanding of curricular aims and practices, but may be blindsided by their own repertoire of teaching strategies. Teachers may believe a particular method or teaching style to be "the best," and not understand that curricular structures are often quite flexible and open to many different, yet effective, interpretations of how to construct teaching. To avoid a sense of "teaching rigor mortis" and develop dispositions of inquiry into curriculum work, Frede suggests that teachers visit other classrooms, and pose questions related to achieving curricular goals. Collaboration with others who are focused on similar curricular goals is seen as an important part of continued growth.

Creative Adaptation. At this phase, teachers understand the "rationale, purposes, and philosophy of the curriculum well enough to adapt it to very different situations, environments, and children" (Frede, 2003, p. 22). These teachers can work in many different situations and do not rely on a particular teaching methodology. They are highly capable of adapting the curriculum to individual needs of students, and their work may be or appear to be intuitive. Teachers at this stage of development often make good mentors, since their understanding of curriculum and practices contains both depth and breadth.

What is important about Frede's characterization of career growth and development is that it ascribes career growth and development to *self-analysis, reflection,* and developing professional *conversations* with others. Her model clearly shows how teachers can focus their energies on specific problems and then alter their actions toward productive ends.

TAKE ACTION 3.1
Interview a Beginning Teacher

The purpose of this Take Action is to gain general insights into the ways beginning teachers learn to teach. Spend some time with a teacher who is in his or her second or third year of teaching. As you observe and prepare for your interview, focus on some of the ideas that Frede suggests as characteristic of teachers in different phases of learning. Below are some ideas to help you begin.

Mastering the Nuts and Bolts

- What classroom structures do you feel are most important for creating a productive learning environment?
- What structures, after reflection, did you reject and jettison? Why?
- How has your thinking about planning changed from when you first started? What are some things about planning that you wish you had known when you first started that you now know as a matter of reflection?
- What do you think are the most realistic and attainable set of skills that a new teacher can work toward?

Too Much of A Good Thing

- What one teaching strategy really seems to work for you? Or, what one or two strategies do you turn to regularly in your daily interaction with students?

- If an observer were to say that you were excellent at a specific teaching approach, what would it be? Why? What would the observer identify as missing from your teaching repertoire? And what recommendations do you think he or she might make to you in order to expand your repertoire?
- How would you describe your teaching style? What do you think are the strengths of your style? What are its weaknesses?
- How do you avoid falling into a "one size fits all" kind of thinking when you teach a specific concept or skill?
- What would be five questions that you would ask yourself that would get you thinking about your interactions with students?

Do it My Way

- When you chat with other teachers about strategies that are different from your own, how do you reconcile differences?
- In what ways does a curriculum allow each teacher creativity and flexibility in teaching?
- If you could visit another classroom on a regular basis, what questions would you pose to the teacher about achieving curricular goals?

Creative Adaptation

- How does your teaching approach change and stay the same when you work with different groups of learners?
- What challenges in the classroom require the most creative adaptation on your part?
- What teaching principles or curriculum rationales seem to cut across all learning situations? How do you adapt strategies to meet the needs of students, while at the same time staying in alignment with your principles and beliefs?

The Teacher Career Cycle: A Closer Look at Lifelong Learning and Development

"The Teacher Career Cycle" model of teacher development proposed by Ralph Fessler (1992) suggests an approach quite different from the model offered by Ellen Frede. After examining practicing teachers' self reports that explored a range of ideas related to teaching, students, and the profession in general, Fessler proposed an eight-component career development model with the following elements: pre-service, induction, competency building, enthusiastic and growing, career frustration, stable but stagnant, career wind down, and career exit.

Fessler's model is dynamic and flexible, and not solely dependent upon a linear progression from one stage to another. That is, a teacher may move from one component of the model to another depending upon environmental influences associated with personal and/or organizational factors. For example, getting past a personal crisis or responding to a critical life incident may affect a change. In addition, a teacher's family support or her personal outlook on a personal issue may trigger movement. Organizational factors related to a specific school culture—its rules and regulations or the management styles of administrators, agendas and leadership of professional organizations, community and parent expectations, relationships with colleagues, union involvement, or public sentiment and trust in schools also affect change.

Despite the flexibility of the model, there is a sense of progression in the overall scheme in that teachers start out in a preservice period, then move to an induction period, and then to a "professional" period in their lives, and finally move into some kind of career exit. Thus, age and experience, along with contextual/environmental factors, contribute to development. Figure 3.1 shows Fessler's characterization of the dynamics of the teacher career cycle.

Fessler's model allows us an opportunity to gain a greater understanding of the experiences of teachers in different places in their careers. Let's take a closer look at Fessler's model starting with the induction component or phase.

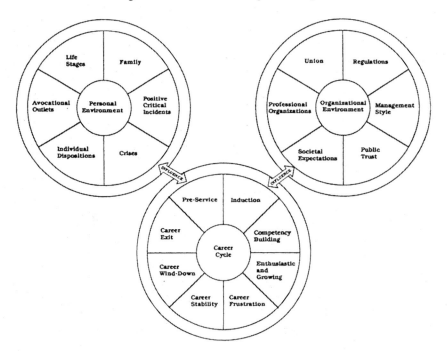

FIGURE 3.1. Dynamics of the Teacher Career Cycle.
Originally published in R. Fessler, Teacher career cycle (pp. 21–44) in R. Fessler & J. C. Christensen (Eds). *Teacher career cycle: Understanding and guiding the professional development of teachers.* Needham Heights, MA: Allyn & Bacon, 1992, p. 36. Reprinted with permission from Ralph Fessler, Copyrighted © 2009, all rights reserved.

Induction. The induction component incorporates the first few years of a novice teacher's employment. This is the time in which teachers are "socialized into the system" or acculturated into the beliefs, myths, and mores of the teacher/teaching community. In teacher mythology this stage is often called "reality shock." During this time, acceptance by peers, students, administrators, and supervisors ranks high in novice teachers' concerns. Achieving comfort and security through the resolution of everyday problems is also a high-ranking concern. Issues related to the induction stage may also occur when experienced teachers move to a new school, shift grade levels or change to a completely different school district.

Competency Building. During the competency-building phase of development, the improvement of teaching skills and abilities are front and center. Teachers actively seek out new materials, methods, and approaches. Attending workshops, trying out new ideas, and enrolling in graduate programs are markers of initiative seen during this time of development. The job remains challenging, and most teachers are eager to improve. Building competence is fundamentally about "getting a handle on things."

Enthusiastic and Growing. Key markers during this aspect of teachers' careers are enthusiasm and high levels of job satisfaction. Teachers possess a high level of competence in their jobs and seek continuing opportunities to improve their teaching. Enthusiastic teachers exhibit the professional and personal traits that we might call "master teachers." They receive and focus on positive reinforcement from their personal environments and in turn make positive contributions to their work environments. According to Peter Burke and John McDonnell, this should be the "target stage" for all teachers (1992, p. 151).

Career Frustration. The attitudinal and personal characteristics that mark this feature of a teacher's career make it seem quite different from the earlier building periods of growth. This is a very critical period in teachers' lives. Much of what people call "teacher burn out" is often associated with the way stress, frustrations, and disappointments manifest themselves during this period. It is also a time when few options may seem available for change, and a time for feeling locked into a position that seems to provide no new rewards. Renewed attention, enthusiasm, innovation, and change of working conditions are necessary for helping teachers regain a greater sense of productivity, place, and purpose.

Stability. Although no one set of terms describes this aspect of teachers' career development, several characteristics seem to stand out. One idea that has interest is the notion of increased expertise. Here enthusiasm and the pursuit of excellence are clear and apparent. A second and contrary idea is concerned with the notion of resignation or even bitterness. Here teachers do what is expected, which may be acceptable, but little more, and are usually not committed to the pursuit of excellence. Stagnation is apparent. Disengagement from their commitment may also be occurring. To stave off the ill effects of career stability, teachers need opportunities for renewal, novelty, and avenues for experimentation that they can control.

Career Wind-Down. The characteristics that mark career wind-down are reflective of the ways teachers have dealt with their previous career development. In the most positive scenario, teachers are getting ready to leave the profession, and see their time as having been pleasant, rewarding. They reflect on the many positive influences that they have had on others. They are also looking forward to change in their lives. A less positive scenario is one where teachers are forced to leave and resent termination, so that bitterness often results. A more "neutral" scenario may be one in which teachers have mixed emotions about leaving, but understand the necessity for change. This is the most unpredictable period in teachers' careers.

Career Exit. This period occurs after teachers have left the profession. No clear path marks the life journeys of teachers after they leave the classroom. Some teachers leave the classroom never to think about it again. Others move into different careers, some education related, others not. Some focus on family, social groups, or other significant people in their lives. All have different plans.

Fessler's model of the Teacher Career Cycle suggests a number of things for the life-long learning process of teachers. Fundamentally, professional growth is personalized and influenced by the professional context in which teachers find themselves. Clearly the concerns of a preservice teacher (as we discovered in Chapter 2) are qualitatively different from a teacher in the midst of competency building or career stabilization. Different attitudes, knowledges, and skills are needed at different times of life, just as different attitudes, knowledges, and skills are needed when we find ourselves in different and sometimes very contrasting school and social environments. What is important about Fessler's description of career movement is recognizing the role that *negotiation* plays in working through different challenges teachers face as they mature personally and professionally.

TAKE ACTION 3.2
Looking into the Future

This Take Action asks you to create a mental picture of what you think or suppose might happen in your future career using two contrasting state of affairs. After thinking through what your situation might look like and how you might feel given these two scenarios, generate a personal development process that uses goals to propel you forward.

Scenario 1. Imagine that you have suddenly been projected into the future 15 years. Based upon your reading of Fessler's teacher career cycle, where do you think you might be? Let's say that you would be in the target stage of "enthusiastic and growing." What kinds of things would you be doing to show that you were growing in your knowledge and skills of teaching people music? What kinds of professional activities would facilitate your growth or hinder it? What actual teaching competencies could you list indicating that you had achieved a high level of proficiency? What would your colleagues be saying about your positive contributions to your working environment, your community, and professional organizations? What goals would be driving your continued development?

Scenario 2. Now, let's flip the coin. Let's imagine that 15 years in the future you find yourself very frustrated in your career. The rewards seem small compared to the energy spent, and stress seems like a daily condition. Disappointment seems to come around every corner. However, there is still hope in your thinking that music teaching is still a "good thing." What kinds of working conditions do you think are necessary to help you regain a sense of productivity, place and purpose? What kinds of personal revitalization goals might be articulated to help you feel that you really can make a difference? What personal action plan could you make to work your way out of your frustrations?

Prepare a brief presentation to share in class or with a small group that addresses the issue in both scenarios and contains your goals for moving you forward in your career.

Library Article Search

Spend some time on-line or at your university library looking for articles on teacher burnout. The *Music Educators Journal* has devoted several articles to the idea of music teacher burnout. Choose an article, and briefly summarize the main points. Try to identify influences that contribute to burnout. What suggestions are provided for dealing with teacher burnout or with the issues that may contribute to frustrations in music teaching? Share in class.

From Novice to Expert: A Closer Look at How Expertise Develops

David C. Berliner (1994) has investigated the differences between expert and novice teachers and has developed a heuristic (or problem analysis) model to explain how expertise in teaching develops. Berliner's model describe fives stages of expertise: Novice (stage 1), Advanced Beginner (stage 2), Competent Teacher (stage 3),

Proficient Teacher (stage 4) and Expert (stage 5). In short, expertise is acquired primarily through experience coupled with the ability to link knowledge gained from experience to the generation of new knowledge in new situations.

Novice. According to Berliner, the primary goal of the novice teacher is to gain experience. Berliner's depiction of novice teachers portrays them as rather inflexible and conforming to rules and procedures. For example, novices tend to apply rules almost regardless of context—"wait 60 seconds before seeking a response" or "never criticize a student." The key set of experiential knowledge to be gleaned is the facts and features of given situations. "Real-world" experience is considered to be much more important than any verbal information.

Advanced Beginner. As experience is gained, novices become advanced beginners. What distinguishes the advanced beginner from the novice is a more sophisticated knowledge base from which to operate. In this stage, teachers become more aware of the importance of context, and begin to recognize similarities across different contexts. As context begins to guide teaching actions, *strategic knowledge*—when to ignore or break or follow rules—is developed. Case knowledge is accumulated. Advanced beginners, however, may not be able to take full responsibility for their classroom instruction because of their focus on trying to "make sense" out of varying classroom events and contexts. As more experienced is gained, and as a teacher willfully chooses what to do, a sense of personal agency develops. Second-and third-year teachers are likely to be in the Advanced Beginner stage of expertise.

Competent Teacher. Two features mark the characteristics of competent teachers: (a) they make conscious choices about their actions, set priorities and decide upon plans, and have sensible means for reaching their goals; and (b) while enacting their goals, competent teachers "think on their feet"—determine what is important or not, attend to or ignore something, decide when to stay on or move off a topic, and make few timing or targeting errors. Because their skillfulness is driven by context, they have more control over events around them, and follow their own plans. Competent teachers tend to feel more responsibility for what happens in their classrooms. Although not very fast, fluid or flexible, competent teachers tend to be more emotionally involved about their successes and failures than novices or advanced beginners. Many third- and fourth-year teachers reach this level. Some teachers, however, remain "fixed" at the competent level of expertise.

Proficient Teacher. Around the fifth year of teaching, individuals advance to the proficient level of development. What separates competent teachers from the proficient ones are several abilities: (a) the ability to pull upon rich case knowledge as a source of information for analyzing teaching and solving problems; (b) the ability to view situations holistically and intuitively; and (c) the ability to recognize similarities across disparate events and see patterns that allow for prediction.

Expert. Expertise, like all the previous stages, is marked by qualitatively different ways of thinking and doing things. As Berliner notes, "If the novice is deliberate, the advanced beginner insightful, the competent performer rational, and the proficient performer is intuitive, we might categorize the expert as often being arational" (1994, p. 10). Experts do things that "work," and appear to do so effortlessly, gracefully, and with fluidity. Their intuitive grasp of a situation almost always is manifested in ways that appear the most apropos. Much knowledge is tacit when problem solving and when things do not go as planned, deliberate analytical thought is brought to bear on the situation.

Berliner's model of expertise and its development is to a large extent dependent upon acquiring subsets of thinking and action skills within a context-rich and bound environment. Experience and reflection on experience are two key components in developing expertise. Simply enacting personal beliefs based on past experience as a guide for future action, however, is not enough and may be "mis-educative" in acquiring expertise. Analysis and reflection must be ongoing and built upon a continuous process of collecting case information. Thus acquiring expertise in teaching is a matter of learning to:

- recognize and interpret classroom phenomena
- discern important events
- judge the typical from the atypical
- enact efficient and routine behaviors
- predict and pre-empt actions
- feel personally responsible or emotionally related to teaching.

TAKE ACTION 3.3
Learn from the Experts

Think of someone you know who is an expert at teaching. What kind of information about teaching do you think she knows that you do not? In his research, Berliner references the importance of case knowledge as a key component in developing expertise. For example, he notes that experts are able to pull upon their accumulated knowledge of individual cases, and build patterns across seemingly disparate situations. Experts see how things that appear to be very different are actually quite connected. They use this "built up" knowledge to predict how something might go in the classroom and plan accordingly. Ask an expert to:

- Describe an important and memorable case in his teaching experience and how it influenced his thinking and actions.
- Define good teaching in terms of lesson structure and teaching strategies.

- Describe how she might make an interpretation of a classroom event (e.g., a student misunderstanding a concept, or a student missing a "final" concert), and the significant contextual clues she might draw upon in generating ideas about the situation in question.
- Explain what lies behind really wonderful, fluid, comprehensive and "evidently effortless" teaching.
- Give details about how he makes himself aware of specific behavioral clues students send in order to change his approach and maintain the flow of a lesson.
- Discuss how she "diagnoses the day." In other words, ask your expert teacher to discuss how she makes judgments about how events, situations, or a day's occurrence might transpire given her perceptions and understanding of a particular set of students and what she has planned for their learning.

TAKE ACTION 3.4
Developing Your Expertise from Case Analysis

This Take Action asks you to learn from your own leadership roles as a basis for developing your thinking across different cases. Think about a series of situations in which you had a leadership role—the lead student in a project, a teaching assistant, a director of a student-run performing group. Jot down as much as you can about the situation's events; place the events in chronological order. Choose a particularly *memorable moment* from each event—one that can act as a catalyst for thinking about expertise. Describe what was significant about it and write a summary statement about what the moment "taught you."

Case Building

Repeat the case analysis process at least two more times. Try to select a different leadership role each time.

Constructing Action Plans

After you have completed writing about several different events, compare and contrast each of the memorable moments. Reflect on what each event "taught you." What similarities can you draw across each one of the cases? What connections can you build between these different events? What "lessons" can you say you learned? How will this analysis help you develop your own expertise?

TAKE ACTION 3.5
Identifying Expertise in the Professional Literature of Music Teaching

The purpose of this Take Action is to conduct a professional literature search specifically related to music teaching and learning. Spend some time on-line or at your university library looking for articles on music teacher expertise. The following journals and periodicals in music teaching learning have published a number of articles on teacher expertise.

Bulletin of the Council for Research in Music Education
Journal of Research in Music Education
The Choral Journal
The Instrumentalist
General Music Today
Journal of Music Teacher Education

Select and read one or more articles. What does the article discuss about expertise? What were the important findings, ideas, interpretations? What ideas on expertise seem similar to Berliner's developmental description? What ideas appear to be distinct? Share in class.

The Lives of Teachers: A Closer Look at the Potential for Positive Development and Transformation

Since the 1960s Michael Huberman and his colleagues have been looking at the lives of teachers and have proposed a theory concerning career life cycles. Huberman's work is an important model for the way teacher research can be conducted, especially in its use of in-depth and open-ended interviews. According to Huberman (1989, 1993) teachers face a number of crises or problems and issues in their professional lives that must be resolved as their careers unfold. How teachers respond to these problems can either lead to growth and development or disengagement from teaching. Thus a "positive resolution" to issues is necessary for positive development to occur. Huberman uses both *themes* and *phases* to describe the process of how teachers work through these issues and the possible actions that can be taken to resolve them.

Themes of Survival and Discovery/Stage of Exploration and Stabilization.
Survival and discovery are the two themes that mark entry into the profession. A pre-occupation with self ("Am I up to this teaching thing?"), along with questions about instructional and classroom management issues typifies the survival theme. The discovery theme conveys the enthusiasm and idealism that comes with having one's own students, classroom, materials, and program. Survival and discovery

might also be thought of as the twin poles of classroom life—there are the often frustrating aspects that come with the "daily grind" and complexities of a job and the satisfying realization of ideals that go along with making something worthwhile and rewarding, such as "making a difference" in students' lives.

Another way to look at these two themes is through the lenses of exploration and stabilization. That is, teachers almost always seek balance in their work lives and try to develop a sense of constancy or stability. Teachers in this early part of their careers work toward developing resources that help them deal with or confront the problems arising out of their interactions with students, other teachers, administrators, and the wider school community. The primary crisis for teachers in this phase is that of *role identification*. Assuming the functions of teaching—the activities and actions that are required or expected of teachers—indicates positive growth. Thus, "acting like" and "thinking like" a teacher are key behaviors and dispositions. In his research, Huberman noted that teachers who felt personally satisfied with their careers over the long term made subjective choices to *commit* to teaching and to *affiliate* with an "occupational community" early on.

Themes of Commitment/Stage of Experimentation/Activism. Commitment is the hallmark of teachers who have successfully negotiated the first stage of their careers. During this second stage, rather than just trying to get the "teaching part right," teachers now begin to focus on student learning. As instructional repertoires become more solid, teachers begin to experiment, often coming to realize that some environmental influences and institutional barriers will have a constraining effect on their impact. The primary crisis that teachers face in this stage of experimentation and activism is that of *continuing commitment*. "Taking stock" of oneself and working through self doubts are key in developing a greater dedication to the profession. Some teachers, for example, may assess that it is time for a career move. Some may move into administration, while others may leave teaching altogether. The key question that teachers must face is: "Is teaching what I want to do for the rest of my life?"

Themes of Serenity and Distancing/Stages of Conservatism or Regret. The last theme to emerge in a teacher's career path is that of serenity. If teachers have made a strong commitment to stay in the profession, they often look for and demonstrate renewed energies, and direct it toward student learning. They appear "composed" and often take on a more "relaxed" approach to class activities. Teachers at this stage have a greater sense of confidence and self-acceptance, although they physiologically may have less energy. They tend to be more introspective and reflective, and may "distance" or remove themselves from school activities. In some cases, distancing leads to greater instructional conservatism—perpetuating methods and approaches that are comfortable for them, but not necessarily appropriate for student learning. Distancing may also lead to regret, the idea that one must retire. Although the "joy of teaching" may be present, the realities of age are pressing.

As we have noted throughout the chapter, studying the career trajectory of teachers is an important way to examine the different issues that may arise at different times during professional development. The study of teacher development allows us to look at how teachers personally shape their own growth and how they are shaped by forces outside them. Some key influences include fatigue, stress, creativity, insight, commitment, disengagement, learning, and reflection. Huberman's work is especially instructive in helping us look at the positive features that are most likely to contribute to a personally satisfying and satisfactory career. In Huberman's analysis, teachers who felt personal satisfaction later in their teaching careers tended to have undergone the following:

■ A concern for instructional efficiency to obtain both learning (achievement) and relational (positive student–teacher) effects. These were teachers who "tinkered" with new materials, different pupil groupings, and made small classroom-based changes, such as revising or changing grading systems, selecting right materials for particular situations, or carrying out curricular experiments.

■ Self-initiated role shifts when they began to feel stale. These were teachers who every four or five years sought a grade level change, or moved from one subject matter focus to another, or changed to teaching more of one kind of class than another.

■ Extended experience with significant results in their classrooms. These were teachers who felt that they had extended periods, even years, in which apathetic pupils came alive, or that their classrooms buzzed with purposeful activity. In many cases these teachers also made major shifts in their instructional approaches.

Overall, it appears that lifelong personal career satisfaction may be strongly linked to three larger ideas:

■ personal efficacy or our own sense of being able to bring about an effect of some kind, and strong role identification,

■ pedagogical artistry and its continuing refinement coupled with a strong commitment to teaching,

■ "renewal"—reflection and seeking change within self and system, transforming existing habits of thinking.

TAKE ACTION 3.6
Thinking Forward—Creating a Renewal Plan

Recall Take Action 3.2 (Looking into the Future) where you had to respond to two imaginary scenarios. This Take Action continues in the same train of thought but is more akin to a "thought experiment." The sciences (and philosophy) sometimes use "thought experiments" to think about problems and the ramifications of interventions in the world without actually intervening. Thought experiments begin with imagined events or scenarios and then call upon our rational thought processes and intuitions in light of what a theory predicts.

To get started, think about the ideas of personal *efficacy* (effectiveness), *artistry* (skill and imagination), *renewal* (regeneration) and *agency* (action) in professional development. Use these ideas as a framework to guide your thinking in the scenario that follows.

Scenario. Imagine for a moment that you are one of the teachers Huberman describes who is reassessing his or her career. You are in your twelfth year of teaching high school band. This is the second school district in which you have taught. You were at your first school for two years where you really learned the ropes, got the routines down and gained a sense of how to be an effective teacher. In your current position, your concert band has garnered numerous county and state awards, toured and even been asked to perform at several prestigious events, including your state governor's inauguration. Student membership is strong, recruitment is of marginal concern, and you have wide community support. A new music teacher might even look at your current position and say "Wow, what a dream job! Have you got the 'gig of a lifetime'!"

However, there is something that is filling you with self-doubt. You feel a bit "stale" in your teaching approaches. Somehow the current way you are teaching just doesn't seem to fulfill you. Your teaching, although good, has become routine and predictable. The issues that nag you are not problems arising out of interactions with administrators, students, other teachers, or even the wider community. The main issue seems to be that of continuing commitment and your belief in making a sustained impact on student learning. It has even crossed your mind that leaving teaching might be OK. Some kind of teaching-focused renewal is needed.

Intervention. What interventions might be appropriate in this scenario that would help bring about a sense of renewal in teaching? What are some specific actions that need to occur to produce a greater sense of empowerment or self-efficacy and reduce self-doubt?

Make a list of interventions (actions and strategies) and their targets (teaching empowerment, teacher self-efficacy, confidence, artistry, or other).

Let's say that you wanted to document a renewal process. Perhaps you could create a "renewal portfolio" to exhibit to others your efforts, achievements, progress and sense of accomplishment. What collections of works or things might you consider as "evidence" to show that renewal has taken place? Consider generating a Table of Contents that shows an organized list of topics contained in your Renewal Portfolio. Underneath each topic, you may want to include a summary of the content to be found, along with illustrative examples.

Teaching as a Lifelong Career: An Expanded Perspective

In this chapter we have encouraged you to expand your initial view of teaching and learning through the process of looking at teaching as a lifelong career. We noted that a teacher's professional development could be examined through several interpretative frameworks, each providing a slightly different view. A theme to emerge in looking at lifelong career development was the strong possibility that frustration and struggle were likely to be part of professional growth. It is likely that you will experience many frustrating times during your teaching, with each frustration dependent upon a host of factors and/or influences. Although we cannot dismiss or eradicate negative or frustrating experience in our careers, we can exert significant control over how we react and respond to problems. Similarly, we found that change is not something that "just happens" to us; we are not passive victims to circumstances that seem beyond our control. We can be active agents in the change process, and can initiate changes in our teaching lives by incorporating new ways of thinking that make professional growth and learning better, more relevant. Acquiring expertise, as Berliner has suggested, is as much a matter of willingness as it is a matter of skill.

We close this chapter on learning from others by tuning into the voices of two teachers: Kristen and Melinda. Kristen's narrative involves looking at several concerns that have emerged during the early years of her career. What distinguishes Kristen's narrative from the previous discussion of concerns in Chapter 2 is the specific identification of the source of her struggles, as well as her own sense of agency in coming to terms with her concerns. As you read Kristen's narrative, pay attention to her directness, her efforts to negotiate conflicting expectations, her determination, and the details of her action plans. When you finish reading Kristen's story, prepare a list of questions that you would like to ask her if she were able to speak to you today.

AT CLOSE RANGE 3.1
Kristen—Removing Roadblocks—Shifting Expectations

As I come to the end of my second year teaching elementary instrumental music, I think back on the concerns I had at the beginning of this job and how they have changed up to this point. When I began teaching, I was deeply concerned with content and method of instruction. I developed a curriculum during my first year that addressed these concerns. I was always thinking about what I wanted my students to know, experience, and how best to help them achieve certain goals. Coming straight from a Master's program where I had developed a progressive philosophy of music education, I tried to build a program that was heavily student-centered and focused on how people learn rather than on teaching straight out of method books and teaching directly toward upcoming concerts.

Several key ideas were important in my work with students: (a) Student-invented and iconic notation as means to understanding conceptually the idea and need for notation—before direct instruction and use of standard notation in a method book, (b) performance of student compositions as an equal partner to performance of traditional band music, (c) process of engaging in music over the development of a musical product.

In hindsight, I was quite idealistic and unaware of the "realities" of teaching instrumental music in the public schools where "tradition of tradition" is quite heavy and pervasive throughout the school. I took risks that may have been perceived as foolish by the more experienced, or perhaps stupid by the more jaded. I never suspected the resistance I got from colleagues and administrators regarding my ideas. I was unprepared to justify what I was doing in the classroom in the face of tradition. Although, philosophically and pedagogically, I knew and felt my approaches were in the best interest of the students. Now, I am concerned with how I can create an honest way of dealing with these pressures without jeopardizing my career. My greatest concerns and anxieties are related to communicating with administrators, parents, and colleagues who do not automatically identify with or share my philosophy of music education. Here are my concerns and goals:

Concerns

- *Articulating my music education philosophy and its implications for pedagogy and content to a non-musician administrator. The principal I have now has developed a clear image of what she wants in an instrumental music teacher based on what she knows. That is performing "familiar music," having a very structured music lesson, using an organizational system to keep track of student achievement and assignments, using the method book sequentially. I believe she sees me as a new teacher she needs to mold. Plus I believe she cares more about whether I can "take her direction," more so than what I know and value.*
- *How to justify with confidence any "non-traditional" methods of instruction I use to a more traditional music educator, or parent or student who has had traditional music instruction.*
- *How to build support for a more progressive and "reform-minded" music education program.*

Goals

- *Project the image my principal wants to see in order to build her trust and confidence in my abilities. Have begun to do so already by doing everything she has told me to do, once I realized that the matter was not open for discussion and that I was in a tenuous situation as a non-tenured teacher.*
- *Once I feel she is completely happy with what I am doing and is confident in my abilities, begin to discuss matters of pedagogy, backing it up with written*

facts, findings, and thoughts of experts in the field of music education. This would be done in tandem with or perhaps after I have done the following:

- *Build a more unified district music department that visibly projects its music philosophy.*
- *Talk more frequently with the elementary general music teacher about our philosophies and pedagogies through the framework of "sharing ideas and helping each other grow as teachers." Discuss how we could possibly collaborate on a project that would help each of us to clarify what and how we teach.*
- *Continue talking with the middle school/high school instrumental music teachers about our philosophies and practices and ask for their support and help in communicating with my principal.*
- *Encourage the development of a district-wide music department sense of community and mission—meet regularly to talk about music education issues and develop a district-wide music education philosophy that supports what we do. Find ways to communicate our philosophy and curriculum as a team to the board of education, parents, administration (my principal in particular), and the community.*

- *Improve communication with parents and community:*

  - *Invite parents to conference with me on parent/teacher conference days—discuss their child's progress, what their child is learning, the instrumental music program in general, and answer any questions/concerns they may have.*
  - *At concerts, set up an area that showcases more student work that is not an "obvious" part of instrumental music programs, such as journal entries, creative work using student-invented notation, recordings of student work that illustrate the collaborative composing process.*
  - *Develop and implement an "informance."*
  - *Make a CD recording of student compositions and distribute it to board of education members, administrators, and parents.*
  - *Submit student-composed melodies to a program that arranges them for orchestra and produces a recording.*
  - *Continue to submit highlights of what my students are learning and doing to school district's parent–community newsletter.*

In her eighth year of middle and high school instrumental music teaching, Melinda has come to a different place in thinking about good teaching from where she started. As you read her story, notice how her points of view were and have been transformed. For example, how did she get from one conception of music teaching to another? What kind of teacher education program do you think created her initial image of teaching? Also notice how she has assumed a new frame of reference for thinking about her self and her work with students. Perhaps, we can wonder as to the kinds of professional development and personal experiences that have contributed to her refashioning of teaching? How does your image of teaching and learning compare with Melinda's? It is interesting to consider how Melinda's thinking implies a whole new set of roles, relationships and actions that are different from her undergraduate preparation. If she were your cooperating or sponsor teacher during your student teaching, what kinds of experience do you hope she would create for you?

AT CLOSE RANGE 3.2
Melinda—Letting Go

My thoughts on what makes a good teacher have changed drastically since my undergraduate training. My teacher training focused mostly on skills, and as a result, I believed a good teacher was one who was highly skilled musically, able to diagnose and "fix" errors efficiently in a rehearsal, and one who had the ability to break down musical skills sequentially to address various age and ability levels of students. I also believed it was someone who could maintain good classroom discipline, and create a context where students were learning, motivated, and (although I would not have used this term then) controlled. I viewed myself as someone who was bringing knowledge to children, and therefore needed to be best informed in musical knowledge, skill and ways of instruction. Training—the word itself—truly seems an apt description of what I experienced and what I believed was the hallmark of a good teacher—someone well-trained. What I believe makes a good teacher now are not qualities having to do with content or classroom systems, but qualities that deal with interpersonal relationships, and acknowledge the subjectivity of both teachers and students, qualities that allow one to create knowledge with children.

We talk of teachers, students and classrooms as if there is one general picture of each, yet every teacher, student, classroom and school is comprised of various identities, in various community and school settings. And because those contexts are continually changing, there is never one right answer in teaching. A good teacher is someone who acknowledges just that, is flexible and reflective, who can continuously reflect on her context, determine the best practice, structure, content and pedagogy for her classroom at that time, and be willing to experiment with various solutions to best meet the needs of all involved. This requires humility, a willingness to question the status quo and transform.

Current school structures and systems place students and teachers in opposition through various hierarchies and power dynamics. A good teacher is someone who tries to resist these dynamics, and acknowledges all of the experience, knowledge and diversity that each student brings to the classroom. Students are not empty receptacles to be filled with our knowledge, and must be seen as people who contribute to a community of learners. A good teacher is someone who not only acknowledges student perspective, but celebrates it and incorporates the students' wealth of knowledge and experience into classroom and curricular goals and pedagogies. Allowing students more of a say in their own learning, and acknowledging them as subjects or individuals rather than objects, allows for powerful learning communities. A good teacher strives for this, and is comfortable "letting go" of the power that school systems expect us to have over student learning.

In Chapter 4, we take a close look at the program structures and conceptual orientations that guide teacher education. Sharon Feiman-Nemser's (1990) five orientations to teacher education (academic, personal, critical, technological, and practical) are used as a framework for understanding how programs, and the experiences of preservice teachers in these programs, differ. Our goal here is to inform and to cultivate a more critical stance toward your own preparation as a music teacher.

For Your Inquiry

Bullough, R. V., Jr. (1989). *First-year teacher: A case study***. New York, NY: Teachers College Press.**

This book discusses the details of a single teacher's development during her first year of teaching, including among other things, an in-depth look at instructional decision making. According to Kerrie, the teacher, what helped most in coping with the problems she encountered was being able to talk about her teaching on a regular basis with someone who was interested in listening. See the follow up on Kerrie's development below in *"First-year teacher": Eight years later.*

Bullough, R. V., Jr., & Baughman, K. (1997). *"First-year teacher" eight years later: An inquiry into teacher development***. New York, NY: Teachers College Press.**

This is a follow up to the 1989 study by Bullough (*First-year Teacher*) and includes the teacher of that study as a co-author. From depictions of the "daily grind" of the classroom to discussions on the "moral center" of teaching, a more engaging and compelling story of professional development would be hard to find. This ten-year collaboration between a practicing teacher and teacher educator is as stimulating as it is unique in the literature of teacher development. Together they tell an extraordinary tale that touches on the meanings of "what counts" in education, the significance of "expertise" in teaching and the importance of professionalism. Moreover, each of their ideas is re-interpreted as beliefs change and experience accrues.

Schoonmaker, F. (2002). *Growing up teaching: From personal knowledge to professional practice***. New York, NY: Teachers College Press.**

Growing Up Teaching follows a single teacher, Kay, from her years of teacher preparation in college through her time as a seasoned veteran. Concentrating on personal knowledge and its influence on teacher growth and development, this 10-year study offers an in-depth and intrinsically appealing image of teacher development. Challenging traditional ideas about theory and practice, teacher retention and pedagogical renewal, *Growing Up Teaching* offers invaluable insight for both the preservice and inservice teacher seeking to develop a strong commitment to teaching.

Hammerness, K. (2006). *Seeing through teachers' eyes: Professional ideals and classroom practice*. New York, NY: Teachers College Press.

What sources of inspiration help sustain teachers' commitments, motivations, and care for their work? How do teachers use their ideals to inform their practice and their learning? Karen Hammerness suggests that teachers have images of ideal classroom practice which she calls "teachers' vision." Through the stories of four teachers, Hammerness provides a path for helping new teachers articulate, develop, and sustain their visions while they navigate the gap between their visions, their daily work, and the realities of school life.

Lieberman, A., & Miller, L. (Eds.). (2001). *Teachers caught in the act: Professional development that matters*. New York, NY: Teachers College Press.

Drawing upon the thinking of a diverse set of contributors, Lieberman and Miller provide both theoretical and practical accounts for deepening the teaching profession's understanding of professional development. Essays focused on student learning, data driven decision-making, personal learning, among others are used to illustrate the relational nature of teacher development. A framework of Contexts, Strategies, and Structures is used to tie together the various ideas used in the text to discuss professional development.

four
Orientations to Teacher Preparation

I am myself plus my circumstances and if I do not save it, I cannot save myself.
Jose Ortega y Gasset, "To the Reader," *Meditations on Quixote,* 1942

A philosophy [curricular orientation] is characterized more by the formation of its problems than by the solution of them.
Susanne K. Langer, *Philosophy in a New Key,* 1942

To foresee future objective alternatives and to be able by deliberation to choose one of them and thereby weigh its chances in the struggle for future existence measures our freedom.
John Dewey, *Human Nature and Conduct,* 1922

FOCUS

In Chapters 1, 2, and 3 you began the process of examining your educational and musical histories, uncovering deeper understandings of your own beliefs and ideas about teaching. You have explored teaching through learning from and listening to the voices of others in the profession. We have challenged you to expand your images of teacher development, understanding that while perspectives of professional growth are fluid and changing, your status as an active agent of change will allow you to be intentional in how you choose to shape your career as a music teacher. As an active agent, you have already made an important choice by selecting the music teacher education program in which you are now enrolled. The goal of this chapter is to assist you in better understanding your current preparation as a music educator. We will examine various orientations to teacher preparation, looking at the various components of your teacher education program and the implications of those components for your continuing development of images of teaching and learning, and for your work as a music educator.

Getting Started

Choosing a university or college to attend can be a daunting task. You have already faced this challenge. You have narrowed your list of educational options, and you have made your decision and are now an active member of a music education course. The program in which you are enrolled has specific goals for graduates of the program, and although the stated goals for music education programs at various institutions may look very similar on paper, the actualization of those goals may create highly varied experiences for the students. Consider the following scenario.

PROLOGUE 4.1
Roundtable at the Mentoring Breakfast

Jim took a sip of coffee as he listened to the animated conversation buzzing around the meeting room. The seventeen first-year teachers at the state conference mentoring breakfast appeared eager to talk about their experiences. Jim, a string teacher with 12 years experience working between a middle school and high school, relished the opportunity to serve as a mentor to first-year teachers. Prior to this year, the demands of his schedule had not allowed him to participate in this relatively new mentoring program, but he had been eager to do so. He remembered vividly the challenges of the first year or two of teaching and how he might have benefited from connecting with another string teacher.

Jim made his way to a table as the coordinator of the mentoring breakfast asked the first-year teachers to find seats at the tables. "As you find your places, please sit with people you do not already know. We want you to have the opportunity to network with other new teachers in the state, and to have the chance for some informal discussion over breakfast before we begin to talk about the opportunities you will have as you participate in the formal mentoring process. There will be one or two mentor volunteers at each table, so take the next 30 minutes to enjoy your breakfast and get to know each other."

As everyone eventually found seats at the tables, five new teachers joined Jim. To begin the conversation, Jim suggested they introduce themselves by giving their names, where they completed their undergraduate degree, and a brief description of where and what they were teaching. A young lady named Candice began.

"Hi. I'm Candice Williamson. I graduated from Tech, and I teach in Columbia. It's a very small town in the northern part of the state—a very rural area. I am THE high school music teacher—I do both band and choir." The young woman sitting next to Candice introduced herself as Grace Wang. *"I went to school here at the U. I teach about 90 miles northwest of here in Fairview. I teach at the high school and do the choirs and I also teach a general music class—sort of like a music appreciation class."*

"I have actually been to Fairview," the young man sitting next to Grace continued. *"I'm Sheldon Watkins, and I went to State. I grew up in the western part of the state, and I'd drive through Fairview going between home and school. Now I teach about 15 miles from here out in the 'burbs at East Middle School – I'm the band director there. I have separate sixth, seventh, and eighth grade bands and I'm hoping to start a music class for students who want to learn the basics—basic theory, but some music appreciation too. Grace, I'd like to talk with you more about your general music class at the high school and how that's set up. Maybe we can visit later."*

Grace nodded in agreement. *"Sure. I struggled with that class this year to try and make it interesting for the students. I didn't have any model for that in my student teaching, or in any of my observations either. That's one of the things I'm hoping to get some ideas for today. I'd love to talk with a teacher who has a really successful class like this."*

Chris Barton, a young man to the left of Grace, joined the conversation. *"My family moved a lot when I was growing up, but we moved here to the city when I was a junior in high school. I ended up going out of state to Northern University, but I knew I wanted to come back here to teach. I'm the band director at Central High School . . ."* Grace interrupted him. *"Really? Wow. I've heard that's a tough school."* *"Well, yes, it's challenging, but someone has to be there and give those kids a chance."* He briefly paused, sipping his coffee. *"I wanted to be there . . . but there were times when I didn't know if I was having any kind of impact. I'm still not sure, but I think I may have made some progress this year and I'm going back next year."*

Jim nodded at the last person at the table for her to continue the introductions. *"Hi. I'm Louisa Richter, and I guess I'm the only one from out of state. I went to the University of St. Charles, which is a private university out west, but we have a lot of relatives here in the southeast part of the state, and that's how I ended up applying for a job in Pleasant Valley. There are three elementary schools there, and I was hired for the general music opening at Washington Elementary."*

Jim's curiosity surfaced, wondering particularly about how Louisa's experience out of state at a private institution compared to those who had attended public universities both in and out of the state. *"What stands out when you think about your undergraduate music ed program? Did you feel prepared going into the classroom last fall? I'm sure you had concerns going into a new position. Were there sometimes when you felt like you needed more information or wished you had had more experiences to prepare you?"*

Sheldon spoke first. "I finished my program feeling very confident as a musician, but I wished I had felt more like a teacher. As far as I'm concerned, I had some of the best theory and history teachers around. Don't get me wrong—I can't say I loved it at the time, but they really made us work, and I know my history and theory! Our aural skills classes were demanding but they made sure we were thoroughly prepared." Grace asked how many semesters of music history were required at State.

"Four—twelve credits total. And that doesn't count the world music class we took. As far as my trumpet lessons, my teacher was pretty incredible. My senior recital was definitely a highlight for me. I love performing and I feel really confident as a musician and in my knowledge of music. I just wish I had felt that same level of confidence the first day of classes last fall when I stepped up in front of my middle school bands. I would have probably felt more comfortable if I had been teaching a high school theory class or a music appreciation class." Grace jumped in, "But you did have the regular music ed classes and the observations and all, right?"

"Sure. I had concert band and marching band methods, and an elementary methods class. But they were in my last year, since most of the music ed classes came right at the end of the program. You probably know this, but State's music ed program is a five-year program. The first four years the focus is almost entirely on what it means to be an excellent musician. We actually were in schools very little until we student taught at the end of the fifth year. I know the state has a minimum number of hours we were supposed to observe, which we did, but there really wasn't an emphasis on that. Our main time in schools was during student teaching. My cooperating teacher was pretty good, but it seemed like the students didn't know as much as they should as far as understanding the music, and I didn't get to do as much with history and theory as I wanted. This year, in my own band room, I had the students do some really great music history and theory projects . . . at least I thought they were great. I don't know—the students didn't seem to get into it like I thought they might. It just seems so important to me that they understand the background of their music and how it's organized—you know, just have a solid knowledge about what they're doing. That was so much a part of my undergraduate work, and I want my students to be prepared if they go on to major in music. I know they're just middle-schoolers, but it's not too early to start. And it's easy for me to teach the history and theory aspects since I feel so comfortable with that. That's why I'd like to start a music theory or appreciation class of some type. Like I said, I wished I had felt as comfortable on the podium!"

Louisa joined the conversation. "Maybe it's because I was at St. Charles, but my experiences seem to be quite different. We had music ed classes from freshman year on, and from the very beginning our professors challenged us to think about our own experiences in schools—the things our teachers had done, what they were like, why our best teachers stood out to us, what we thought was 'good' teaching . . . things like that. 'Reflection' was a word we learned right away! Our professors frequently reminded us that 'learning is in the reflection,' and particularly reflecting on our own experiences, like I said. They wanted us to know what we believed about teaching and how students learn and what should be taught. They helped us to understand that what we believe about being a music teacher is what determines how we teach. Dispositions was a word we quickly came to understand. Basically our disposition about inclusion, for example, comes from what we believe because of our experiences. If I hadn't been challenged to think about this, I don't know that I would have recognized some of the skewed notions I had about inclusion. Another interesting thing we did was to create metaphors of teachers, classrooms, good teaching—it was harder than it sounds because you really do have to think first about what you believe and then to think about how you can communicate it to someone else so they can capture the essence of your beliefs."

"What about observing and going out to the schools?" Again, the question came from Grace.

"We were in schools with teachers early on. I remember interviewing a teacher that I had observed. I saw him do all these interesting and innovative things to get the students to involve themselves in the music . . . I thought he was great. But he was very different from my high school choir teacher, and I had always thought he was the best! I think it was when I was interviewing this teacher that I began to understand that great teaching doesn't have to look the same, and that I didn't have to try to be a clone of any of my former teachers. I could use my strengths and what I was coming to believe and value about good teaching and music education, and become my own version of an excellent music teacher. I'm sure I'll be learning about teaching for the rest of my career, but I feel like I have the tools to know how to reflect on who I am as a teacher and how to keep challenging myself."

"Well, the reason I asked about observations is that getting into schools was a huge part of what I did as an undergraduate." Grace paused for a last bite of her danish and then continued. "We observed everything—general music, orchestra, band, chorus . . . and at different schools. We had an elementary practicum where we taught one day a week in an elementary music class—that was just built into the course requirements of one of our methods classes. Then the semester before we student taught our choral methods class spent most of the time at a school. Our professor would come out to the school with us, and we would all plan together with the choir director for what we would do. The choir director was terrific—she shared so many ideas and gave us great ideas about repertoire, sight-reading materials—her way of interacting with the students was really amazing. But overall, we got to see and experience a lot of different classrooms, which is so important. Each classroom is certainly its own world, and being able to learn things from each of the teachers we observed . . . it was wonderful! Granted, I may not know as much about the research behind teaching," as she looked at Candice, "and I certainly didn't have the emphasis on the core classes like Sheldon, but I felt fairly confident going into the classroom."

Candice quickly jumped back into the conversation to comment that she, too, had many opportunities to develop teaching skills. "We spent a lot of time teaching, but most of it occurred in our methods classes." Looking at Sheldon, she remarked, "Like you, we did our observation hours but we didn't have the variety of experiences that it sounds like you did, Grace. We did a lot of microteaching in our classes where we would teach each other—sometimes just a rote song to practice the process, sometimes any topic but demonstrating our skill with complete teaching cycles. In band methods, we had a lot of podium time, and we would be videotaped and then we would do self-assessments . . . and sometimes the other students would do the assessments. We worked a lot on developing our skills with teaching cycles, delivery skills, those types of things."

Sheldon looked a bit puzzled and inquired about what she meant when she referred to teaching cycles. She laughed as she responded. "It was what we did all the time! Our professors emphasized that all the teaching skills we were learning were research-based and shown to be effective for student learning. Teaching cycles are when the teacher gives a directive or comments, the students respond by doing or following-through on the teacher's directive, and the teacher then gives feedback of some type. There's more to it than that, but in a nutshell that's it. And delivery skills were things like eye contact, non-verbal communication—all the things research tells us makes the difference between mediocre teachers and really effective teachers."

Louisa inquired about the self-assessments. "What were the assessments like? Did you write reflection papers?"

"Occasionally we included reflection papers, but we usually used a checklist the professors gave us. Part of it included things like score preparation, knowledge of the music, and so on, but it also included things like eye contact, body language, use of questioning techniques, . . . the delivery skills I just mentioned. Anyway, by the time I got to student teaching I had actually done quite a bit of teaching but it was primarily in front of peers in my classes at the university."

Chris had been quietly listening up to this point. The program at Central, where he was now teaching, had seen three directors come and go within the last five years, and as he had stated earlier, he was determined to stay and give the students a sense of continuity. He looked around the table with a curious expression on his face. "So let me ask about something. Did any of your professors discuss political action with you?"

"You mean advocacy? Keeping music in the schools?" Louisa quickly continued. "Sure, we had some discussions about that and I remember that we participated in an MENC webinar about how to advocate for music programs."

"No," Chris replied, "I'm talking about the politics of education. It's all political, really. I mean, look at what poverty has done to the children in this country. Look at how many kids are getting lost and left out in the school systems. We say we have equal opportunity education but it's not equal at all. Where there's money, there's power . . . at least that's been the case, and it's up to us as teachers to be out there *letting people know that all students in America do not have equal opportunity to learn. The 'haves' and the 'have nots' exist in our country and in our schools it's getting worse instead of better. Prejudice still exists, and racial and ethnic biases are definitely still apparent in our schools."*

"So this was something your professors discussed in your classes?" Sheldon looked somewhat puzzled at this thought.

"It was more than just random discussions. I think they saw it as their mission to make sure we went into teaching ready to question prevailing practices that discriminate, and that we were aware of the hidden curriculum that's in every school and how that affects the students. We were encouraged to be activists— activists in the school by looking for the prejudices and biases in curriculum, in the music, in the way we teachers interact in the classroom, and activists in the community by creating awareness of the ways communities can help level the playing field for all students. Every day I see that race, gender, and class influence the kinds of opportunities and experiences students have in schools. What we really need is social justice in education. If you think about it, change is only going to come if teachers become much more active in taking the students' voices to the administration, the school boards, the politicians . . . it's why I applied for the job I got, and I am determined to hang in there and make a difference for these kids."

"What," questioned Candice, "do you mean by a hidden curriculum?"

"Isn't that like all the unwritten rules that a school has," Grace responded. "I remember that we were supposed to see if we could figure that out at one of the schools where we observed." Chris nodded, agreeing with Grace's answer. "Yes," he replied, "it's all the social and cultural ideas and values that a school thinks are important for the students to learn . . . what they need to be 'successful citizens.' It's not all bad, but when you think about the way society influences schools and teaching, it's all political and we as teachers need to be very aware of what we're expected to implicitly teach the students . . . we shouldn't just go along with business as usual without thinking about what's REALLY happening to the students in the process. I actually did a study for one of my undergraduate classes where I looked at methods books we use with students and all the implicit messages students are sent through those materials. You wouldn't believe . . ."

Although Chris looked as though he wanted to continue this line of discussion, the moderator of the session stood and addressed the group to introduce the guest speaker to give some background to the mentoring program. As the table talk died down and everyone's attention turned to the speaker Jim reflected on the conversation. What had started with a seemingly simple question had turned into a discussion that left him with a very different question. "How did they all, coming through seemingly similar programs, come to have such different undergraduate experiences?"

TAKE ACTION 4.1
Gaining Insight into Teacher Education: Characterizing Experiences

The purpose of this exercise is to identify the defining characteristics of each of the five individuals' experiences in the scenario you have just read. Re-read the discussion and comments of each new teacher in the scenario, and using Table 4.1 as a guide, make a list of the kinds of experiences and learning each first-year teacher mentioned as part of his or her undergraduate program. List the actual experiences each one described, and also list other experiences you may be able to infer from their comments. Include specific learning concepts when apparent.

    Decide what you believe to be the goal of these various experiences. Why would music professors emphasize certain aspects of the program over other aspects? Think about the ways these various perspectives and areas of focus impact the development of teachers' knowledge, skills, and dispositions as you consider possible purposes for the various experiences.

TABLE 4.1 Characterizing Experiences

Teacher	Experiences	Purpose
Sheldon		
Louisa		
Grace		
Candice		
Chris		

When you made the decision to attend the institution where you are currently enrolled, some of the factors you considered likely included the availability of your desired major, the reputation of the university and/or program, geographic location, cost, and financial assistance available. However, what could be argued as the most important factor impacting a program of study is seldom as clearly apparent as the factors listed above. Rarely is a program directly promoted in terms of the theoretical frameworks that guide the experiences within that program. And even though the list of required courses in a program may look very similar across institutions, as Jim noted in the scenario above, the experiences you will have may vary widely from those of students in other institutions. At the core of these varied experiences lies the theoretical framework adopted by the education or music education faculty in their respective institutions. Understanding the framework providing the foundation for your curriculum is important as you synthesize, reflect on, and make meaning of your experiences throughout your collegiate career. This chapter provides an overview of the importance of and impact of those theoretical frameworks—what we refer to as orientations to teacher education, emphasizing the importance of the identification and implementation of such an orientation; a discussion of the identifying characteristics of five major orientations; and our argument for a personal orientation to music teacher education.

Introduction to Orientations to Teacher Education

The nature of a teacher education program is determined both by the structural model and the conceptual orientation that provide the basis for that program. The structural model defines criteria such as the length of the program, the number of credit hours, the configuration of those credits (general, major, professional, etc.), and the number of hours/semesters of field experience. Some initial licensure programs are completed in four years, others in five years. Five-year programs may lead to a bachelor's degree, to a bachelor's and master's degree, or to a master's degree. Credit hours required can vary from 120 to 140 or more at some institutions.

The conceptual orientation of any program reflects specific views of teaching, learning, and learning to teach. The word orientation can be defined as *the position in which something is developed or focused.* Howey and Zimpher (1989) describe a conceptual framework in teacher education as the "cornerstone" of any coherent and cohesive program while Feiman-Nemser (2001) states that a conceptual framework "provides a guiding vision of the kind of teacher the program is trying to prepare" (p. 1023). She has further defined an orientation to teacher education as "clusters of ideas" about the goals of a teacher education program and strategies for accomplishing those goals. As we discuss orientations in this chapter, we are referring to decisions that have been made intentionally to develop a teacher education program reflecting a particular position or focus. It is this conceptual orientation, or theoretical framework, of any teacher education program that guides the faculty in decision-making processes regarding the overall program goals as well as the goals for individual courses, such as the goals you see listed on your syllabi, the types of experiences embedded in the coursework, the nature of assessment, and the culture and contexts for learning, among others. But because only in the broadest sense is there agreement about what future teachers should know and be able to do, these orientations, as exemplified by the novice teachers at the mentoring breakfast, are markedly different from one another.

TAKE ACTION 4.2
Gaining Insight into Teacher Education: Your Professors' Perspectives

The purpose of this Take Action is to gain greater insight into the conceptual orientation of your music teacher education program by conducting an interview with one or more of your professors. Think back to Chapter 2 and the experience of interviewing a teacher in the field. Review the process of interviewing outlined in Take Action 2.1 as you prepare to interview one or more of your professors in the music education program. Again, you will want to identify a particular professor for your interview, and prepare by writing questions.

To better understand your professor's positions and ideas you may want to request a copy of the professor's CV, or Curriculum Vitae in advance of the interview. You may already have this information from your work on Take Action 2.2. If not, this document, in essence a résumé, will provide the professor's educational background as well as listings of all institutions where he or she has taught, courses taught, research/presentations/workshops reflecting his or her line or lines of scholarship, and, in most cases, a list of professional organizations with which the professor is affiliated. Examine the CV and see what you can infer about the professor's perspectives on music teaching and learning as well as his or her ideas about teacher education.

Consider the following questions to include in your interview:

- What aspects of the teacher education program do you feel are most valuable for preservice teachers?
- What specific experiences within the program do you feel are particularly important and why?
- What specific experiences within courses do you value most?
- How do you choose what to emphasize in the courses you teach? How do you decide what to leave out?
- What would you like to add to the current program that you feel might enrich the teacher education program?
- What might be components of teacher education programs that you question?
- What knowledge, skills, and/or dispositions do you most hope your students take with them as they graduate from the program?
- When you are attending conferences and are hearing (formally in presentations or informally in conversation) graduates or current students from other institutions, can you identify the institution where they studied or are studying? Do you see characteristics that distinguish graduates from certain institutions?
- Who is the "[institutional name]" graduate? What makes graduates from this institution distinctive?

- What are the values of this program?
- What does this program most value in its students?

Write a summary of your interview. Send a copy to the professor you interviewed for confirmation of accuracy. If revisions are needed, reconfirm the report with the professor after making the necessary changes. When it is completed, compare your interview with interviews conducted by other students. Does it seem that the professors share very similar perspectives? What are commonalities? What are differences? As a class, you may want to create a chart or map of the categories that emerge from similarities and distinctions found as you compare the outcomes of the interviews.

If you have the opportunity to do so, schedule an appointment with the Dean or Director of the School of Music at your institution to conduct a similar interview. Do the perspectives of the professor(s) and Director or Dean seem to focus on the same goals? Again, what are the commonalities? What are the aspects or issues where there seemed to be differences in perspectives?

If you are enrolled at an institution where there are a small number of music education professors you may wish to invite the professors to your class for a "group" interview or a panel discussion. Out of professional courtesy it may be inappropriate for your class to ask 2–3 faculty members to respond to several invitations for essentially the same interview questions. Another option may be for you and your classmates to divide into groups equal to the number of music education professors at your institution, with each group interviewing one of the professors. It is always important to be aware of the schedules of those being interviewed and to respect their timeframes for the interview.

Overview of Five Major Orientations to Teacher Education

Sharon Feiman-Nemser (1990) has contributed a great deal to the writings and understandings about orientations to teacher education. She has compared and summarized teacher education frameworks and has found them to be generally reflective of five major orientations: (1) The Academic Orientation, (2) The Technological Orientation, (3) The Critical Orientation, (4) The Practical Orientation, and (5) The Personal Orientation. Each of these provides a differing perspective on what Feiman-Nemser (2001) refers to as the "central tasks" of teacher education. These central tasks, reflecting current thinking about teacher education, include: analyzing beliefs and forming new visions; developing subject matter knowledge for teaching; developing understandings of learners and learning; developing a beginning repertoire of teaching techniques and strategies; and developing the tools to study teaching. Consider these central tasks as you begin to explore the five orientations to teacher education programs. Table 4.2 further clarifies these orientations.

TABLE 4.2 Orientations to Teacher Education

	View of Learning	View of Teaching to Teach	View of Learning	Emphasis within Music Classrooms	Metaphor of Orientation
Academic Orientation	Acquisition of factual knowledge Induction into scholarly disciplines	Transmission of knowledge Development of understanding of subject matter Teacher's role as scholar and subject matter specialist	Clear standards are established for prospective teachers to reinforce mastery of content area Emphasis on teaching the structures of the discipline	Memorizing and possessing factual knowledge Examples: Names of composers, rhythm tree, lines/spaces on the staff, traditional approach to music appreciation	Teacher as scholar
Technological Orientation	Acquisition of skills and procedural knowledge	Use of generic strategies and behaviors found through empirical research to be related to student achievement Development of procedural knowledge Competence is defined by student performance Direct instruction	Amalgamation of sets of discrete skills to prepare students for tasks of teaching Emphasizes need for skills based on teacher effectiveness research Intense observation and feedback strategies Simulated classroom experiences	Emphasis on skill in performing Proficiency Examples: Scales played at 120 mm., hands together	Teacher as technician Teacher as technical trainer
Critical Orientation	Purpose of reform; new social order Awareness of social inequities	Teacher role as educator and political activist Promotion of democratic values Development of group problem-solving skills	Create awareness of school inequalities Help preservice teachers develop awareness of hidden curriculum Create awareness of	Emphasis on empowerment Examination of lyrics for biases and prejudices Emphasis on how people are represented	Teacher as activist

Table 4.2 Continued

	View of Learning	View of Teaching to Teach	View of Learning	Emphasis within Music Classrooms	Metaphor of Orientation
		Activism in both school and community Promoting social justice Help students foster a critical outlook	practices designed to maintain status quo	in musical traditions Concern for equitable representation of diverse musical styles and practices	
Practical Orientation	Highly contextual Whatever works for the particular student in the moment	High level of emphasis on *practical* applications of theory Teachers refine practice through reflection on experience Requires high level of flexibility rather than structured pedagogies	Experience is the best teacher Apprenticeship with master teachers to develop knowledge of the craft Collect materials from experienced teachers Strong emphasis on highly contextual, unpredictable nature of teaching	Emphasis on teacher-tested strategies, materials Ease of use of materials Emphasis on passing down teaching tips Use of songs that hook and motivate Management strategies Familiar warm-ups and practice strategies	Teacher as craftsperson Teacher as practitioner
Personal Orientation	Self- and socially constructed Development of the self and development in socio-cultural contexts Understanding of self	Encouraging and assisting rather than prescribing Facilitator; creates context for learning Student-focused learning requiring knowledge of students and their interests and abilities Understands intra- and inter-personal aspects	Foster notion of teacher as learner Learning, understanding, and developing one's self as teacher – personal development Facilitate students' growth towards self-adequacy Create safe environment to allow risk-taking	Music projects that involve problem-solving Individual, small-group, whole-class Teacher encouraging musical independence Student generated goals and self-assessments Example: Group compositions	Teacher as learner and collaborator Teacher as agent of change

Academic Orientation. The Academic Orientation can be described as promoting a solid emphasis on the academic core in any discipline. This central theme, emphasized in the work of the Holmes Group, suggests that teacher candidates should be engaged in solid academic preparation (subject matter knowledge) followed by an apprenticeship with a skilled teacher. Learning is seen as the acquisition of factual knowledge, and teaching is primarily regarded as transmitting knowledge and fostering understanding of the subject matter. The role of the teacher is that of scholar—being an expert or specialist in the subject matter. Those adhering to an academic orientation generally promote clearly defined teacher education standards.

Think back to the mentoring breakfast scenario and Take Action 4.1. If you recognize Sheldon as being the graduate of a program with an academic orientation you are correct. His emphasis on performance and the core music courses—theory, history, aural skills—suggest a very thorough preparation as a musician. But as he indicated, in this framework the time designated for developing the knowledge, skills, and understandings of educatorship—that is, understanding of the interactions among teacher, learner, subject, and context—does not equate with that devoted to musicianship. He felt this lack of knowledge and skills for teaching when he began his teaching. Although he had strong ideas about *what* he wanted to teach, his ideas about *how* to teach were less defined.

Technological Orientation. The Technological Orientation, exemplified in the scenario by Candice, is rooted in behaviorist theory. This orientation promotes the notion that teacher competence results from attaining sets of discrete teaching skills that have, through research, been associated with high student achievement. The focus is primarily procedural—that of knowledge and skills of and about teaching, learning specific teaching behaviors, strategies, and methods. The programs of competency-based teacher education in the 1970s, focused on teacher effectiveness, exemplify this orientation. In teacher education programs, a primary focus in the technological orientation is the attainment of research-validated knowledge and teaching practices. Often there is an emphasis on microteaching in the preservice methods classes, with feedback through checklists focused on skill development. As you noted in Take Action 4.1, Candice referred to her many opportunities for teaching, but these were almost exclusively teaching her peers in the methods courses rather than working with students in the field.

In the technological orientation, teaching is usually a form of direct instruction and learning is seen as acquisition of specific skills. Competence for both preservice teachers and for students in K-12 classrooms is most often measured by performance or outcomes.

Critical Orientation. In contrast, the Critical Orientation rejects the behaviorist approaches to teacher education and argues for teacher empowerment—that teachers own their knowledge and development as educators. Additionally, social inequities, social/education reform, and democratic values in society and schooling form major themes running throughout curricula based on this orientation. Fostering awareness of the paradox of schooling as both redefining social order as well as reinforcing social inequities becomes one of the central tasks of the critical orientation. The role of the teacher is seen as both educator and activist/reformer. Understanding and engaging in policy making, particularly related to issues of social justice, is a key component of programs based on this orientation.

It is quite easy to identify Chris as the teacher in the mentoring scenario having participated in a program with a critical orientation. Certainly political activism occupied his focus—activism both in and outside the classroom. His awareness of the "hidden curriculum" underscored his concern about social inequities that are actually reinforced in schools. Yet he was optimistic and determined that he could and would create an awareness of the need for social justice, both in and out of schools, and be able to make a difference for his students. Teachers having a critical orientation will most likely be those on committees dealing with school policy and curriculum, and they will be actively engaged in their communities in volunteerism and political activism.

FOCUS ON RESEARCH 4.1
Sex Equity in Music Education. **(A focus issue of** *The Quarterly Journal of Music Teaching and Learning)*

In 1993, a special focus issue of *The Quarterly Journal of Music Teaching and Learning* included several articles that reflect views of authors holding a critical orientation toward music teacher education. In this case, the specific focus was gender equity in music education.

Julia Eklund Koza, guest editor for this specific issue, opened the issue by underscoring the importance of, and need for, gender research. Koza also authored an article (1993) in which she examines gender issues in college choral methods texts. Because these texts are considered "expert knowledge" in choral music education, she wanted to know how gender and gender-related issues were discussed in these texts. This article, drawn from her dissertation work, looked specifically at the problem of a shortage of males in choral music programs. Koza found that less than half of the choral music education texts contained gender references, and of those that did, the vast majority perpetuated traditional gender discourse, which "socialist feminists assert, are at the heart of the different oppressions of women and gay men" (p. 48). Koza concluded her article with a call for challenging the traditional taken-for-granted assumptions regarding gender in music education.

In this same issue, Molly Weaver (1993) looked at higher education and schools of music in her article titled *A Survey of Big Ten Institutions: Gender Distinctions Regarding Faculty Ranks and Salaries in Schools, Divisions, and*

Departments of Music. Weaver found that "for women, the problems of under-representation and inequitable compensation [in higher education] have not gone away" (p. 91).

Patricia O'Toole (1993) used a feminist criticism theoretical framework to look at issues of power and control in a choral music classroom. She believed that "the conventions of choral pedagogy are designed to create docile, complacent singers who are subjected to a discourse that is more interested in the production of music than in the laborers" (p. 65). O'Toole discusses theories of power and the lack of "voice" for the members of most choral groups. She concluded that this is not the fault of the director or singer, but rather the result of a system of traditions of choral pedagogy determining the interactions between director and singer. According to O'Toole, it is that system, based on a power structure and set of beliefs formed from male culture, which must be questioned.

Practical Orientation. Experiential learning and "craft" knowledge form the structural pillars of the Practical Orientation, with the goal of assisting teachers to develop practical ways of carrying out the tasks of teaching. Often including an apprenticeship, this experience-based perspective has sometimes been seen as disconnected from theory and research, although more recent research reveals the positive attributes of situated cognition, or authentic-context learning—the practical knowledge one gains from being situated in a "real" classroom. While programs with a practical orientation can differ widely in some aspects, a shared trait is the understanding of teaching as being highly contextual, and that good teaching occurs with the recognition of the needs of the localized, complex, and shifting context of schooling. In other words, teaching is largely determined by and in response to the needs of each unique classroom. Learning to teach is therefore seen to occur best by teaching in actual school settings, working closely with teachers in the field who have developed "practical pedagogical knowledge" based on their years of experience. This emphasis on context recognizes the need for individual flexibility and creativity and rejects the notion of a generic set of teaching behaviors as discussed in the technological orientation.

Again thinking back to the scenario, Grace discussed what she perceived to be the benefits of having participated in a program based on the practical orientation. She valued the opportunity to interact with "master" teachers in the field, and to have extended experiences in classrooms with "real" students, yet acknowledged that her preparation did not place the same level of emphasis on research-based skills as did the technological orientation, nor the strong emphasis on core preparation as in the academic orientation.

Music teacher education programs espousing a practical orientation may include methods courses at what is known as a professional development site (PDS). A PDS is not a "laboratory school," but rather a classroom in which a school music teacher has agreed to open her class to university students. For example, in the following study, the professional development site was a middle school choral classroom. The methods students met, along with the university faculty member, at the middle school for their methods course, where they worked together with the school choral teacher to plan, teach, and reflect on their teaching. This approach to methods classes exemplifies the emphasis of the practical orientation on experiential learning.

FOCUS ON RESEARCH 4.2
Uncovering Preservice Music Teachers' Reflective Thinking: Making Sense of Learning To Teach

Susan Wharton Conkling (2003) conducted a study to examine the reflective thinking of preservice choral music teachers in a professional development site. Seven music majors (five undergraduates and two graduate students all seeking initial licensure) formed the cohort of students in the study. The orienting questions for Conkling's study were:

- What is the nature of the reflections generated by preservice music teachers who are immersed in teaching at a professional development site?
- What do these reflections imply about music teachers' professional growth and identity development in the initial stages of learning to teach?

The professional development site, where the music major cohort met for two mornings a week throughout the semester, was a middle school for grades 7 and 8. The student cohort, working jointly with the middle school choral teacher and the university faculty member, planned instructional time. They then worked with two seventh grade choirs enacting those plans. Time at the professional development site was also designated for music analysis, reflection on the middle school students' musical learning, and revision of lesson plans.

This study was a collective case study in which Conkling's role was that of participant–observer (both university faculty member involved in the process, and researcher making observations). Data collected for analysis included observation field notes, music students' journal entries, and transcriptions of unstructured interviews with the music students. Pattern analysis allowed the data to be grouped thematically; item analysis related the data to the research questions.

Conkling stated that for the music students participating in this study, learning to teach "was constructed around both the question of 'how is it done?' and . . . 'who shall I be?'" (p. 11). She found that these participants developed their teacher identity and ideas of pedagogy by: looking for expert teacher models, rehearsing or problem-solving in their teaching performance between lessons and classes, and seeking out other educators, particularly their peers in the cohort, for honest feedback and support.

Personal Orientation. Carter and Anders (1996), drawing on the works of Doyle, Feiman-Nemser, and Zeichner, define a personal orientation as "personalized teacher education that focuses on coming to terms with oneself, maximizing a sense of self-efficacy, clarifying one's values, and discovering one's own personal meaning and style in teaching" with "emphasis on teachers' voice" (p. 561). While the personal orientation had its origins in counseling psychology and developmental theory, recent interpretations of this framework have moved it beyond its roots to include a strong emphasis on "reflection, the study and writing of stories and cases, action research, and teachers' life histories, narratives, and personal knowledge" (Carter & Anders, pp. 560–561).

The role of the teacher is seen as that of "learner" and the emphasis is on the *process* of learning rather than solely on developing teaching skills or practices. Important in understanding this perspective is that the teacher-as-learner's primary goal is understanding and developing oneself in ways that help to clarify his or her own beliefs about teaching and learning. A sense of self-adequacy as a teacher is promoted, particularly as it relates to the teacher's ability to know and teach to the needs of individual students. According to Feiman-Nemser, teaching is seen as assisting, guiding, and encouraging, since students share this same need for self-understanding as do preservice teachers and teachers in the field. The teacher is seen as one who facilitates the individual learning goals of each student, guiding each student toward independence as a learner. Creating an environment to foster the attainment of these individualized goals becomes an important focus for the teacher with a personal orientation. The classroom environment reflects a constructivist approach, derived from the students' interests and promotes exploratory, active approaches to learning.

Learning to teach in a program with a personal orientation is viewed as a process of development or "becoming." There is an emphasis on reflection on past experiences in schools to assist preservice students in making sense of the roles of teacher, student, subject matter, and context in the overall process of learning. Louisa made several references at the mentoring breakfast to this idea of knowing one's own beliefs and learning from reflecting on experience. Identification of teaching beliefs is an important part of any discussion of specific topics related to teaching and learning. If you think back to Chapter 1, Focus on Research 1.2 summarized a study about preservice teachers' metaphors, and you created your own metaphor in Take Action 1.6; both of these reflect the personal orientation in assisting you to uncover your own beliefs about "ideal" teachers.

Shifting from thinking like a student to adopting "teacher thinking" is a part of the process of developing as a teacher. Teaching is not seen as a set of discrete skills nor is it adopting methods and strategies demonstrated by other teachers; rather it is viewed as an ongoing process of identifying and developing one's own personal and unique style of teaching. Teacher educators will often focus on guiding preservice teachers through the early teaching concerns of self and task, to a focus on student-centered learning. With this idea of personal orientation in mind you may want to revisit Focus on Research 2.1 and re-read the discussion of preservice teacher concerns.

TAKE ACTION 4.3
Gaining Insight into Teacher Education: Analysis of Programs

Consider the orientations to teacher education that have been presented. Based on your understanding of these five orientations, how would you classify the emphasis or emphases within your current program?

Examine your college handbook and the university website to discover if there is a clearly identified orientation. If not, does your music teacher education program (or teacher education program) have a theoretical model or conceptual framework stating the goals of the program? If the teacher education program at your college or university is NCATE accredited [*National Council for Accreditation of Teacher Education*] you may find the conceptual framework and goals as a part of that documentation. If so, does this model reflect a particular orientation to teacher preparation?

Locate your institution or department's mission statement. Based on your understanding of this statement, the conceptual framework, and the stated program goals, as well as a review of your course syllabi and program of study, what would you identify as the orientation of your program? "Does your program seem to have a clear orientation, does it seem to exhibit a combination of two or more of the orientations, or does it lack a clearly defined orientation?

Think back to Take Action 4.2 and your interview with the music education professor(s). If possible, have a discussion with your professors to gain their perspectives and opinions about these five differing orientations to teacher education.

TAKE ACTION 4.4
Gaining Insight into Teacher Education: Perspectives of Teachers in the Field

Consider the five orientations to teacher education that have been presented. In small groups, work with your peers to construct on a 3x5 card a brief profile of what a teacher who is a graduate of each of these orientations would believe, do, emphasize in their music classes, and how they would interact with students and peers in a teaching context. Share your group's five profiles with the profiles created by the other groups in your class or seminar. Make any adjustment(s) to your profile(s) that you feel help to further reflect the orientation represented.

Contact a music educator in the field and request to meet with that teacher to discuss the profiles you have constructed. When meeting with the teacher, give them the five profile cards describing teachers from the five orientations. You may want to pursue the following lines of questioning.

- What kinds of strengths and weaknesses would each of these teachers bring to a music classroom?
- Who would you want to hire as a colleague? Why?
- Who would you *not* want to have as a colleague? Why?
- What successes do you think each of these teachers would be likely to achieve during their first five years of teaching?
- Which teachers would you project would stay in music education and which ones do you feel might be most likely to leave the profession?

As soon as possible after the interview, write a brief report of your interviewee's perspectives. Did the teacher you interviewed seem to identify with any one of the five profiles? Present your report to the class. Is there consensus among teachers in the field about the importance or impact of any of these orientations? How do the perspectives of the teachers impact your own further understandings about the impact of these orientations?

Important Considerations When Examining Orientations

A caution is important at this time. You have examined your own program and analyzed it in light of the five orientations of teacher education outlined by Feiman-Nemser and others. Yet all those who write and research these orientations are quick to state that it is infrequent that you will find a program that clearly and specifically reflects only one of these orientations. Many programs are combinations of two or more of these perspectives. Programs may seem to lack a clear affiliation with any of these orientations, but elements of one or more may be present when the goals and structures of the program are carefully examined. Individual courses within a program may reflect certain orientations based on the individual perspectives of the professor.

It is also possible that these orientations may be viewed as developmental. Think back to the discussions about teacher development in Chapters 2 and 3, particularly the theory of Berliner [Novice/Expert development] (1994), and Fuller and Bown's (1975) work regarding the seemingly developmental nature of teacher concerns. Certainly the technological orientation may provide the "security" of known and rehearsed skills for teaching that is important in alleviating concerns early in the teacher's development. With more experience as a novice teacher and greater inter-action with other teachers, early professional development experiences might relate to a perspective more in line with the practical orientation. One might consider that a critical orientation plays an essential role in teacher education, but that it could only be realized in classrooms when a basic understanding of context and teaching strategies is already in place. Situational factors may play into the realization of ori-entations. Chris' own background, moving frequently and interacting with stu-dents in a variety of contexts, may have contributed to his choice of a teacher education program promoting critical awareness of social issues.

Just as in any teaching and learning situation, the context of the learning is also a factor that may create variations on the actualization of these orientations. We agree with the proponents of the practical orientation in that teaching is highly con-textual and context bound. Teaching is indeed complex, with the interactions among the teacher, the students, the content of the subject, and the environment creating unique and highly personalized experiences in classrooms. Teaching and learning in higher education is no different in relation to the impact of context. Because of this, it may be presumptuous to believe that these orientations could be enacted in the clean and distinctive ways in which they have been presented in this chapter.

Equally important is to consider, as you may have discovered in your interviews and discussions with the professors in your program, that the individual perspec-tives of each professor are varied, based on their beliefs and experiences in teaching, in higher education, and in their various forms of scholarship. Even in programs with a clear orientation, or a strong conceptual framework, the "carrying out" of that framework will still look different from one course to another based on your interactions with professors, including the ways they approach teaching, learning, the subject, and the type of context they create for learning. It reflects the same way that you, as a teacher, will carry your specific beliefs and perspectives into your classrooms. In essence, everybody has a personal orientation. The question is to what extent that orientation is incorporated in the overall orientation or frame-work of the teacher education program, and to what extent is it apparent in the actual program goals, the courses taught, and the interactions with students both in and outside the classroom.

We have presented these orientations with the purpose of giving you an opportunity to step back and look at your teacher education program holistically—to reflect on the structures and goals in place at your institution. As stated above, teaching is complex, and teacher education is no different. It cannot, realistically nor practically, be broken down into five simple categories. Yet knowing more about the general characteristics of these orientations will allow you to be more thoughtful about the ways that you will identify, understand, reflect on, and synthesize the experiences you are having and will continue to have in the process of your continued development as music educators.

In this chapter, you have analyzed the program in which you are currently enrolled in order to develop an understanding of the structure and goals of the program, and if possible, to identify the orientation or orientations reflected by your program. Perhaps you had never considered before how a program can reflect an overarching set of assumptions. You may be thinking that you would prefer a greater emphasis on an orientation not represented by your program. You may believe that a blending of these orientations would enhance your overall development as a teacher. You are not alone. The perfect teacher education program does not exist. Music education professors, the National Association of Schools of Music [NASM], NCATE, state Departments of Education, and policy makers frequently examine programs of teacher preparation with the purpose of continuous improvement.

TAKE ACTION 4.5
Gaining Insight into Teacher Education: "In the Driver's Seat"

In this Take Action, we ask that you try to step outside your current role and explain your program to someone else. Imagine that you are at the mentoring breakfast. Consider the following questions:

- How would you characterize to someone else your program structure? Goals? The coursework? The types of experiences?
- Is who you are or who you want to become as a teacher congruent with the teacher preparation program you are experiencing?
- What aspects of the program seem to have the strongest influence on your current thinking about teaching and learning?
- What do you feel will be your greatest gain from your current program?
- What are the areas you feel need to be strengthened given your current program?
- In what areas do you feel you will need more guidance as a first-time teacher?

Reflecting on your responses to these questions, consider this your opportunity to be "in the driver's seat" and begin to chart a plan for your personal development as a teacher. Based on your analysis of your own program and your understanding of the core suppositions of the five orientations described in this chapter, create a plan that includes:

- A brief description of the music education and education courses and types of experiences in your current program.
- A list of the types of knowledge, skills, and experiences that you would also like included as part of your program but that are currently lacking or not apparent.

With these two components in mind, consider the ways that you can take the initiative to address what you perceive to be lacking in your program. Create a set of goals for ways you can choose to develop—on your own or with others in the program—the knowledge, skills, and experiences you have identified above. For example, if you are in a program emphasizing a technological orientation, and feel you would benefit from more frequent reflection on your microteaching, or from more time directly with students in classrooms, how might you problem-solve to create these opportunities for yourself? What are positive ways you can approach the concerns you may have about your program?

Based on the goals you have identified, create an action plan. What are practical ways that you can address these goals? Describe what you can do "in the now," what actions you can pursue over the course of this semester, and what will be ongoing aspects of your action plan. Be specific as you determine your action plan.

Discuss your ideas, goals, and action plans with your peer(s). There is a sense of accountability in the spoken word, and often the discussion of ideas with others allows you to in turn support each other in the pursuit of your goals.

Place yourself in a proactive position—a position of personal agency—in setting these goals and in developing the practical means for achieving them. This is a mature perspective reflecting a personal orientation—that of teacher-as-learner. You may recall that in Chapter 3 several of the teacher development theories related professional growth to teachers' initiative and willingness to take on new aspects of learning about teaching. It might be easy to become critical of the program in which you are enrolled as you reflect on the experiences you may believe to be beneficial but perceive to be lacking in your program, but in the analysis of your program, it is important to first acknowledge the strengths of that program. Essential to your development as a music educator is your understanding that education is not something done *to* you, it is a choice you can make. The development of these goals and an accompanying action plan is an excellent process for strengthening your thinking as a teacher as you make choices about your professional development.

Positioning Ourselves Within a Personal Orientation

At this point you will have recognized that we promote the idea of a personal orientation for music teacher education. The process of engaging in Take Action 4.5, and the Take Action opportunities throughout this book, are examples of the ways a personal orientation can be infused throughout any teacher education program. Reflection on past experiences and in present learning contexts, analysis of beliefs, understanding the roots of your assumptions about teaching, developing "teacher thinking," fostering a sense of personal agency as a teacher—these actions may be a choice that you make personally or they may be a focus of your professors and the program in which you are enrolled. In either situation, it is a process of understanding yourself and the impact of your personal histories on your development. We believe that the focus on teacher-as-learner, and the emphasis on reflection on past experience to make sense of the present and to develop understandings for future action as teachers are at the core of becoming the teacher you envision when you think of an ideal music educator.

In looking ahead to Chapter 5 we will take Feiman-Nemser's idea that learning to teach is "learning to understand and use oneself effectively," and further develop this perspective, including the idea of change and reform in education. You will have opportunity to reflect on your own sense of personal agency—the ability to make choices about how you will "become" and "be" as a music educator—and to continue to develop an understanding of the choices that you can make about your own development as "teacher-as-learner."

For Your Inquiry

Academic Orientation

Sedlak, M. W. (1987). Tomorrow's teachers: The essential arguments of the Holmes Group report. *Teachers College Record, 88*(3), 314–325.

Technological Orientation

Bowers, J. (1997). Sequential patterns and the music teaching effectiveness of elementary education majors. *Journal of Research in Music Education, 45*(3), 428–443.

Duke, R. A. (1999). Measures of instructional effectiveness in music research. *Bulletin of the Council for Research in Music Education, 143,* 1–48.

Duke, R. A. (2005). *Intelligent music teaching: Essays on the core principles of effective instruction.* Austin, TX: Learning and Behavior Resources.

Hendel, C. (1995). Behavioral characteristics and instructional patterns of selected music teachers. *Journal of Research in Music Education, 43*(3), 182–203.

Yarbrough, C., & Price, H. E. (1989). Sequential patterns of instruction in music. *Journal of Research in Music Education, 37*(3), 179–187.

Practical Orientation

Conkling, S. W., & Henry, W. (1999). Professional development partnerships: A new model for music teacher preparation. *Arts Education Policy Review, 100*(4), 19–23.

Critical Orientation

Frierson-Campbell, C. (2006). *Teaching music in the urban classroom, Vol. 1: A guide to survival, success, and reform.* Lanham, MD: Rowman & Littlefield.

The July 2007 issue of *Music Education Research* presents a collection of articles focused on topics of social justice and equity. The issue includes articles such as:

Frierson-Campbell, C. (2007). Without the 'ism: Thoughts about equity and social justice in music education. *Music Education Research, 9*(2), 255–265.

Jorgensen, E. R. (2007). Concerning justice and music education. *Music Education Research, 9*(2), 169–189.

Reimer, B. (2007). Roots of inequity and injustice: The challenges for music education. *Music Education Research, 9*(2), 191–204.

Personal Orientation

Campbell, M. R. (Ed.). (2007). Music teacher education special focus issue. *Music Educators Journal, 93*(3).

Thompson, L. K., & Campbell, M. R. (2005). Guides, gods, and gardeners: Preservice music education students' personal teaching metaphors. *Bulletin of the Council for Research in Music Education, 158,* 43–54.

five
Searching for Horizons

Cultivating a Personal Orientation toward Change

A person who knows her own mind—how it learns best—is most likely to be able to change her mind effectively.

Howard Gardner, *Changing Minds*, 2004

Every teacher learning, every day, individually and collectively, is the sine qua non *of transforming schools for educating all and for sustaining society.*

Michael Fullan, *The New Meaning of Educational Change*, 2007

Change in education is easy to propose, hard to implement, and extraordinarily difficult to sustain.

Andy Hargreaves and Dean Fink, *Sustainable Leadership*, 2006

It is what teachers think, what teachers do, and what teachers are at the level of the classroom that ultimately shapes the kind of learning that young people get.

Andy Hargreaves and Michael Fullan

FOCUS

Educational change is the organizing theme of this chapter. Now that you have considered how various orientations to teacher preparation influence the images of teaching that preservice teachers form, this chapter will extend the notion of a personal orientation by inviting you to think of yourself as a change agent.

"Learning to understand, develop, and use oneself effectively" (Feiman-Nemser, 1990, p. 4) requires teachers to move, act, and learn in multiple realms of influence. Exercising your agency also requires clarity of purpose. Various methodologies will help you understand the complex interplay of tradition and innovation in music education specifically and education at large, develop a critical stance about the assumptions of change that accompany reform efforts, reconcile how teachers operate in contexts of constraint and flexibility, and above all, inventory your own ideas about the changes you intend to enact in your classroom. The chapter ends by reflecting on the emotional dimensions of change in teachers' lives and acknowledging the moral nature of decisions that shape teaching and learning.

It Is I Who Must Begin

It is I who must begin.
Once I begin, once I try—
here and now,
right where I am,
not excusing myself
by saying that things
would be easier elsewhere,
without grand speeches and
ostentatious gestures,
but all the more persistently
—to live in harmony
with the "voice of Being," as I
understand it within myself
—as soon as I begin that,
I suddenly discover,
to my surprise, that
I am neither the only one,
nor the first,
nor the most important one
to have set out
upon that road.

Whether all is really lost
or not depends entirely on
whether or not I am lost.
                    —Vaclav Havel

Vaclav Havel has led an extraordinary life. As the former president of the Czech Republic, he led his country through the transition from Communism to democracy. As a playwright and politician, he has drawn upon his artistic sense as a deep source of reflection and wisdom in guiding policy decisions. As a humanist, he has inspired individuals to take action guided by their intuition, experience, and deeply rooted sense of purpose. His commitment to human rights has been widely acknowledged and celebrated. Clearly, Havel has both experienced profound changes throughout his lifetime and acted on his beliefs to bring about change. His significant accomplishments have been grounded by strong moral convictions about freedom, choice, and responsibility.

The determination that this poem conveys also rings true with many who have chosen teaching as a career. Many teachers are dedicated to making a difference in students' lives; many selflessly act on these beliefs to craft a satisfying life in teaching. Recall your thinking in Chapter 1 about the attributes of successful teachers. In addition, reflect for a moment on the extraordinary teachers you have known and those who have been particularly influential in your decision to pursue teaching yourself. How would you characterize their commitment and sense of purpose? There are numerous themes in Havel's poem—a sense of agency, connection to others, and above all, a very strong capacity for seeking improvement—that many exemplary teachers regard as essential dispositions to ground their work in classrooms. Overall, this poem captures one very important aspect of educational change—that change often begins with individuals who are committed to making a difference, and who use their beliefs as a compass to take action and to craft a professional identity.

Change is a ubiquitous characteristic of teachers' lives. We believe that the way music teachers understand the elements and processes of change is essential to their growth, as well as the growth of music education in schools and communities. Now more than ever, teachers' work is played out against a backdrop of changes that originate both inside and outside the classroom. For a number of historical, technological, sociological, political, and ideological reasons, the rate and degree of change in schools and society has accelerated in the last few decades and will continue to do so. This chapter will help you develop and refine your orientation toward change by engaging you in methodologies that we hope will lead to personal insight and a strong sense of your capabilities to effect change in music classrooms and schools in general. First, however, we must take some time to think about aspects of teaching and learning that seem resistant to change.

Rip Van Winkle awakes...

There's a dark little joke exchanged by educators with a dissident streak: Rip Van Winkle awakens in the 21st century after a hundred-year snooze and is, of course, utterly bewildered by what he sees. Men and women dash about, talking to small metal devices pinned to their ears. Young people sit at home on sofas, moving miniature athletes around on electronic screens. Older folk deny death and disability with metronomes in their chests and with hips made of metal and plastic. Airports, hospitals, shopping malls—every place Rip goes just baffles him. But when he finally walks into a schoolroom, the old man knows exactly where he is. "This is a school," he declares. "We used to have these back in 1906. Only now the blackboards are green."

(Wallis & Steptoe, 2006, p. 50)

Understanding Tradition and Innovation in Education

Many educational philosophers, historians, and theorists have made the same observation as Rip Van Winkle about aspects of schooling that seem perennial, widespread, and particularly resistant to change. Educational historians David Tyack and Larry Cuban use a linguistic metaphor to describe how schools are infused with patterns of thought, behavior, and organization that are robust and embedded in school life (Tyack & Cuban, 1995). They describe tacit assumptions about teaching and learning and the way schools operate as the "grammar of schooling." Just as we use grammatical patterns in conversation without paying attention to parts of speech, verb tenses, and sentence construction, teachers learn to teach by acting in agreement with implicit rules for interacting with students, presenting content, assessing learning, and transmitting cultural values. Learning to teach involves socialization as these rules become accepted as "just the way things are done." Consider the accompanying photograph (Figure 5.1) as you read this quote from *Tinkering toward Utopia: A Century of Public School Reform:*

> The basic grammar of schooling, like the shape of classrooms, has remained remarkably stable over the decades. Little has changed in the ways that schools

FIGURE 5.1. Evidence of the Grammar of Schooling.

divide time and space, classify students and allocate them to classrooms, splinter knowledge into "subjects," and award grades and "credits" as evidence of learning. (Tyack & Cuban, 1995, p. 85)

Some of these patterns help us define the very concept of *school* and the process of *education* but even these strong pillars and foundations need to be inspected regularly for cracks and crevices. John Dewey wrote about another very common perception of educational change—that various ideas swing in and out of favor like a pendulum swings from side to side—and offered a possible solution for teachers to break free from the cycle:

> The tendency of educational development to proceed by reaction from one thing to another, to adopt for one year, or a term of seven years, this or that new study or method of teaching, and then swing over to some new educational gospel, is a result which would be impossible if teachers were adequately moved by their own independent intelligence . . .
>
> If teachers were possessed by the spirit of an abiding student of education, this spirit would find some way of breaking through the mesh and coil of circumstance and would find expression for itself. (Dewey, 1904, p. 16)

Dewey understood how teachers can become tangled in webs of comfortable habits, familiar cycles, and well-established routines. "Breaking through the mesh and coil of circumstance" implies that teachers need to analyze and disrupt educational patterns that are no longer suited to the realities of the classroom. Many teachers might agree with Dewey that they are often conscripted to adopt some new "educational gospel," as each year brings with it some new program or initiative they are asked to adopt. Few innovations last as long as the seven years Dewey mentioned; one year is hardly enough time to reset old patterns of interaction so that the change is a lasting one.

The processes of reflection, inquiry, and dialogue with critical friends often leads teachers to uncover and speculate on these resilient grammars of school life, which can also hold true for particular fields such as music teaching and learning. Exercising an "independent intelligence" enables teachers to break free as change agents in school settings. Dewey's quote is consistent with the idea of teacher as learner, in that teachers who are "possessed by the spirit of an abiding student of education" will see their classrooms and school settings as places for conducting inquiry and for questioning their beliefs and practices. As a new teacher, you may be entering the field excited by the chance to reshape music classrooms according to innovative ideas that have occurred to you; however, you may also value and wish to preserve the traditions and characteristics of the field that attracted you to music education in the first place.

Another way that you might think about grammars of schooling is through the examination of historical artifacts. The photographs on the following

FIGURE 5.2. First Grade Pupils of Dayton's Irving School, 1958.
Photo from p. 55 of article by G. H. Zimmerman, "Everyone Wants To Be Wanted,"
Music Educators Journal, September–October 1958. Copyrighted © 1958 by
Music Educators National Conference. Reprinted with permission.

FIGURE 5.3. Springfield, MO, Public Schools Television Classroom, 1959.
Photo from p. 70 of article by L. L. Lewis, "The Story of the Hagerstown ETV
Project," *Music Educators Journal*, September–October 1959. Copyrighted ©
1959 by Music Educators National Conference. Reprinted with permission.

pages were taken from the *Music Educators Journal* to show various classroom settings and students. What evidence of music teaching and learning do these photographs portray that is still as true in contemporary classrooms as when the photographs were taken? Which aspects of music teaching and learning may have changed?

At first glance, you might see these photographs as fairly common scenes in which children move creatively to music or an ensemble performs for the public. If you walked into schools anywhere near where you are now, you might recognize some of these same activities and familiar aspects of music teaching and learning. At the same time, there may be less obvious themes having to do with race, ethnicity, gender, socioeconomic status, technology, and repertoire in these photographs that may capture your attention.

TAKE ACTION 5.1
The Grammars of Schooling and Music Education as You Have Experienced Them

Make a list of the patterns of school experience that you think would be good examples of the "grammar of schooling" that Tyack and Cuban describe. Think first about schools in general, and then make another list to describe the "grammars" of music programs. To begin, it may be helpful to concentrate on the physical set-up of classrooms, the typical responsibilities and behaviors we associate with teachers, the way school schedules are configured, the kinds of work and responses that are expected of students. You might also prompt your thinking by asking some simple questions: Who talks? Who listens? Who decides what should be discussed? Who asks questions? Who answers them? What are some common routines? What happens when routines are disrupted?

For music, it might be helpful to describe the common features of an ensemble setting, such as their elective status; solo, small group or large ensemble festivals; chair placement; or the typical flow and structure of rehearsals. For general music classes, you might focus on common activities, expectations for performances, scheduling, or student attitudes toward general music. Compare your list with others, and identify common patterns, as well as those that are distinctive to particular settings.

Before you continue reading, take time to make a list of the directions for change that you think are most important for music educators to pursue. In what ways do you think the profession of music education might break free of traditions that need to be revised and redirected? Which traditions deserve to be preserved and maintained? *Who* should decide? *How* do you decide?

Perhaps as you acted on your knowledge about the grammars of schooling, you may have concluded that as a teacher relatively new to the field that you are not yet influenced by patterns and traditions—both obvious and subtle. Recall, though, Dan Lortie's notion of the apprenticeship of observation you encountered in Chapter 2. If what is known about teaching is formed through one's experience as a student in school contexts, it makes sense to uncover and confront these robust images of how music teachers think, act, behave, and interact with others. Lortie writes of these challenges in helping beginning teachers reconcile their preconceptions with the norms of the field:

> Teachers have been shaped in turn by their own teachers and by their personal responses to those teachers—such influences stretch over many years. The result is an accretion of views, sentiments, and implicit actions that may be only partially perceived by the beginning teacher. Whatever can be done to help future teachers make implicit dispositions explicit will free them to become more aware of what they do while teaching and to more readily consider practices to which they have not been previously exposed. (Lortie, 2002, p. xi)

It sounds as if it is quite difficult to break free from ways that young teachers are socialized into the routines of the profession before they are hired for their first positions. Eunice Boardman addressed the very thorny problem of "teaching as you were taught" in her 1985 address to the Society for Music Teacher Education. She urged music teacher educators to break the cycle by working to close the gap between theory and practice:

> We are victims of our own learning for we tend to teach, not as we were taught to teach, but as we were taught. And thus the gap between what we know—theories of teaching and learning which have resulted from research, experimentation, and observation—and what we do—the teaching behaviors readily observable in the classroom—continues to widen. (Boardman, 1985, p. 66)

A strategic way to develop your skills of observation and reflection on the structures and patterns that are embedded in schools and classrooms is to examine what reformers, critics, or individuals with promising ideas think teachers should be doing differently. Often, these calls for change are framed as a way to encourage teachers to move *away from* tired and worn assumptions and routines *toward* more educationally sound beliefs and practices. A book commonly recommended for teachers was written by Steven Zemelman, Harvey Daniels, and Arthur Hyde, and titled *Best Practice: Today's Standards for Teaching and Learning in America's Schools* (2005). These authors combed through reports of various professional societies and associations related to curriculum in math, science, social studies, English, and the arts to compile common recommendations to guide changes in teaching and learning. As you read this list, note how many of these recommendations for change may be reflected in the content of your teacher education curriculum as well (recalling from Chapter 4 how teacher education program orientations vary along several dimensions.

TABLE 5.1 Common Recommendations of National Curriculum Reports

LESS whole-class, teacher-directed instruction (e.g., lecturing)	MORE experiential, inductive, hands-on learning
LESS student passivity: sitting, listening, receiving, and absorbing information	MORE active learning in the classroom, with all the attendant noise and movement of students doing, talking, and collaborating
LESS presentational, one-way transmission of information from teacher to student	MORE diverse roles for teachers, including coaching, demonstrating, and modeling
LESS prizing and rewarding of silence in the classroom	MORE emphasis on higher-order thinking; learning a field's key concepts and principles
LESS classroom time devoted to fill-in-the-blank worksheets, dittos, workbooks, and other "seatwork"	MORE deep study of a smaller number of topics, so that students internalize the field's way of inquiry
LESS student time spent reading textbooks and basal readers	MORE reading of real texts: whole books, primary sources, and nonfiction materials
LESS attempts by teachers to thinly "cover" large amounts of material in every subject area	MORE responsibility transferred to students for their work: goal setting, record keeping, monitoring, sharing, exhibiting, and evaluating
LESS rote memorization of facts and details	MORE choice for students (e.g., choosing their own books, writing topics, team partners, and research projects)
LESS emphasis on competition and grades in school	
LESS tracking or leveling students into "ability groups"	MORE enacting and modeling of the principles of democracy in school
LESS use of pull-out special programs	MORE attention to affective needs and varying cognitive styles of individual students
LESS use of and reliance on standardized tests	MORE cooperative, collaborative activity; developing the classroom as an interdependent community
	MORE heterogeneous classrooms where individual needs are met through individualized activities, not segregation of bodies
	MORE delivery of special help to students in regular classrooms
	MORE varied and cooperative roles for teachers, parents, and administrators
	MORE reliance on teachers' descriptive evaluations of student growth, including observational/anecdotal records, conference notes, and performance assessment rubrics

Note: Compiled and adapted from S. Zemelman, H. Daniels, & A. Hyde (2005). *Best practice: Today's standards for teaching and learning in America's schools* (pp. 4–6). Portsmouth, NH: Heinemann.

This is quite an extensive list of educational moves. As you read this list, could you identify the general orientation of many of the recommendations—towards more constructivist practices, sociocultural theories of learning, or progressive ideals, for instance? What does this list have to say to teachers in settings where standardized tests are the primary measure of student achievement? For many teachers, recommendations like these create a steady and some might say unrelenting expectation for change, particularly when recommendations turn into requirements that impact daily decisions about content, instruction, and assessment. You might also conclude that real change is rarely as tidy as this list might suggest. In reality, most teachers work in the territories between more traditional practices and more innovative practices, figuring out just how to respond and deciding whether calls for change fit their own desires and intentions for their classrooms.

TAKE ACTION 5.2
Less and More for Music Education

Although Zemelman, Daniels, and Hyde cite the *National Standards for Arts Education* as one of the documents they consulted to derive this list, return to the recommendations in Table 5.1 and mark ones that seem especially fitting for music classrooms. What other moves from *less* to *more* can you develop that convey proposed reforms in music education? For example, you could cite recommendations to move from traditional emphases on large ensembles to more chamber groups, diverse smaller ensembles such as mariachi or African drumming, or musically creative work in composition, arranging, and improvisation. From individual lists, compile a comprehensive list of recommendations that reflect the consensus of small groups or the whole class.

As an extension, you can show the lists to music teachers in the field to initiate a conversation about proposed reforms from their points of view.

Understanding Change Processes

The study of educational change is a field in itself, often marked by the publication in 1971 of a book by Seymour Sarason titled *The Culture of the School and the Problem of Change*. Some of the leading figures in this field include Michael Fullan, Andy Hargreaves, and Matthew Miles (See **For Your Inquiry** at the end of this chapter for more suggestions). Their work is of interest to those outside of the classroom who seek to change schools from a systemwide vantage point as well as to those within classrooms who have a more intimate and ongoing relationship to change proposals.

Since the very concept of change has so many meanings, work in this field clarifies the locus of change (whether the impetus for a new idea or practice comes from *outside* the school or springs from the ideas of those *inside*); the scope of change (having to do with the settings in which the change is to be implemented—ranging

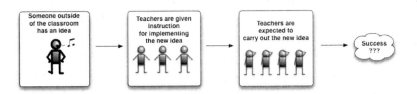

FIGURE 5.4. An Empirical–Rational Approach to Change

from classroom, particular schools, clusters of schools, entire subject areas, widespread policy to be enacted for all schools); and the content of change—the specific area or areas of teaching and learning to be addressed.

Virginia Richardson and Peggy Placier are two researchers who have studied teacher change extensively. They describe one of the most common models of educational change, called the empirical–rational approach (see Figure 5.4).[1] In this approach, individuals outside of a particular school context act as change agents by conducting research or developing an innovative program that promises an improvement in teaching and learning. Teachers are informed of this innovation, and are given instruction in implementing the new strategy or practice. Administrators, staff developers, or researchers expect that the teacher will carry out the new strategy in the classroom in order to obtain the desired outcome or result, such as improved student learning. This approach operates under the assumption that teachers are "the recipients and consumers of research and practice" (Richardson & Placier, 2001, p. 906). The locus of change is initially motivated by reformers outside the classroom, and the expectation for change is that teachers will effectively implement the new idea that the reformers have described.

The empirical–rational approach to educational change has a longstanding history, but not particularly a distinguished track record. As you might imagine, there might be a number of reasons to explain why these change initiatives have often failed to make the significant differences that the change agents hoped would happen. A particularly important study conducted by Mary Kennedy investigated the extent to which teachers actually implement the strategies that reformers propose.

FOCUS ON RESEARCH 5.1
Inside Teaching: How Classroom Life Undermines Reform

Mary Kennedy (2005) conducted a study of 45 upper elementary school teachers in schools undergoing reform. In her book, *Inside Teaching: How Classroom Life Undermines Reform,* she sought to uncover the teachers' point of view on reforms generated outside of the classroom.

Kennedy set out to test five hypotheses for the failure of many reforms to effect significant change in classrooms. The five hypotheses were:

1. teachers need more knowledge or guidance in order to alter their practices;
2. teachers hold beliefs and values that differ from reformers' and that justify their current practices;
3. teachers have dispositions that interfere with their ability to implement reforms;
4. the circumstances of teaching prevent teachers from altering their practices; and
5. the reform ideals themselves may be unattainable or may actually impede practice. (Kennedy, 2005, p. 12)

Kennedy used an interesting method to study her participants, making two videotapes simultaneously as they taught a lesson of their choice. One videotape was given to the participating teacher, and one was kept by the researcher. Teachers were asked to select teaching episodes that were interesting and important, and to prepare for an interview with the researcher in which these episodes would be shown and described. The researcher did the same with her copy of the videotape. After the participating teacher described the episodes she had selected, the researcher used the excerpts she had chosen to probe and extend the thematic focus of the interview. This method, called "stimulated recall," provided rich data for the researcher to examine.

Kennedy found wide variations in the way that teachers implemented reforms in her study, but several findings in particular are of interest here:

- Teachers who altered their beliefs and practices to reflect the new knowledge promoted by the reform made significant changes in their classrooms, and they often interpreted these new ideas in ways that made their working theories of teaching and learning more powerful.
- Teachers who met new challenges with a calm and steady disposition were also more responsive to the new ideas suggested by the reform. Although the circumstances of teaching such as scheduling, disruptions, and managerial demands often made it difficult for teachers to concentrate on reform ideals, Kennedy found teachers willing to invest their energies in implementing new ideas in complex and challenging classroom environments. Support structures, however, were needed to prevent these reform-oriented teachers from exhausting themselves.

TAKE ACTION 5.3
Representing a Change Process

Rather than revising the diagram of the change process used in Figure 5.4 to show the normative–reeducative strategy and presenting it for your examination, we invite you to draw your own representation of the change process that starts with teachers' desires and intentions to bring about some lasting differences in their classrooms.

How will you represent a change process that starts from a teacher's desire for improvement, rather than a response to some external requirement or recommendation? Could your diagram address how change is sometimes inspired by the "outside" while also aligning with teachers' intentions? Can your diagram also include support for teachers' implementation of new ideas?

Compare and discuss different approaches to representing change processes, using your diagrams as artifacts for analysis. Can you describe an example of a significant change in your own thinking using this diagram? What do your diagrams reveal about your understanding of change?

The word *reform*, which we have not yet defined, is often used in a specific way. Reform is often framed as a movement or initiative for which the agenda for change is formed by individuals, groups, and policy makers other than teachers. If prescriptions for reform are seen as edicts, trends, or policies to be followed, the teacher's role is that of carrying out prescriptions for action. Walker and Soltis seem to take this perspective when they write "welcome or not, reform is a fact of professional life for teachers, who must find ways to deal with it" (Walker & Soltis, 2004, p. 94). Walker and Soltis continue by describing four stances that teachers take regarding reform. They state that you can: "embrace a reform; resist a reform; adapt a reform to your own purposes; and ignore a reform" (p. 94). Although this is certainly the case, it seems that one crucial question is missing, particularly for teachers who have the desire and capabilities to bring about change. Why not initiate a reform?

The idea that reform is something done to teachers, rather than something that teachers do is quite pervasive when you begin to examine it. One way to turn this problem on its ear is to look to another approach to educational change, called the normative–reeducative strategy (Richardson & Placier, 2001). This approach to change starts with the teacher who engages in deep reflection on her beliefs and practices. Dialogue with mentors or critical friends often assists the teacher as she examines possibilities and consequences of change. The impetus for altering teaching practice stems from the particular needs, characteristics, and desires of the students and teacher. One of the most obvious differences between the normative–reeducative strategy and the empirical–rational approach is in the direction of the change. It is easy to rush to judgment here and say that change that comes from the outside must be suspect, and that change stemming from an insider's perspective is obviously more likely to result in meaningful and lasting results. Certainly, good ideas are likely to come from many sources. Engaging the teacher's beliefs related to the good idea is an essential aspect of implementation. You may also realize that this view of change fits quite closely with the idea of a personal orientation to teaching.

Trends in Music Education

The term *trend spotting* is often used when popular media talk about predictions in clothing styles, new car designs, color trends, or technological gadgetry. When you speak with experienced teachers about changes they have experienced in the span of their careers, you may hear well-worn phrases such as "we've done this/seen this before; just wait until the pendulum swings back; here's yet another bandwagon; this is just the latest trend."

To call something a trend is to suggest that it is transitory and perhaps to hope that it will pass before teachers must choose whether to implement the thrust of the reform. Yet trends in education are powerful forces. Large, complex, and powerful ideas move us along in our thinking, inspire teachers to make changes, and bind teachers of similar interests together in the pursuit of innovative ideas. To some extent, the demands and opportunities of teaching are different for each generation, an idea captured by Andy Hargreaves: "The time of one's life is also intricately connected to the life of one's times" (Hargreaves, 2005, p. 968). For you, this means that certain "big ideas" will appear on the radar of your school agendas at various times in varying ways. If you can prepare to inform your thinking about these contemporary trends, you can decide how meaningful they are for your work in music and for your school at large. This will give you opportunities to think clearly about whether you will follow Walker and Soltis' advice to "embrace a reform; resist a reform; adapt a reform to your own purposes; and ignore a reform" (p. 94). You may also be inspired to create your own reform.

TAKE ACTION 5.4
Becoming a Trend Spotter

Strategies for Trend Spotting

- Launch a media watch. For a specified period of time (a day or a week, perhaps), be alert to the educational issues and problems that are addressed by media (radio, television, general magazines such as *Time* and *Newsweek*, blogs, etc.). What insights does this give you about the way the public at large views educational challenges, issues, and opportunities?

- Analyze trends in educational periodicals. Three periodicals that are often read by administrators, curriculum coordinators, and other school personnel are *Educational Leadership,* published by the Association for Supervision and Curriculum Development; the *Phi Delta Kappan;* and *Education Week.* You can often find issues of these periodicals in teachers' lounges as well as online. Examine the themes and lead articles in recent issues to make a list of current educational trends and topics. For example, recent themes of *Educational Leadership* include Science in the Spotlight, Improving Instruction for Students with Learning Needs, Responding to Changing Demographics, The Prepared Graduate, Curriculum for the Whole Child. Recent themes of *Phi Delta Kappan* include The Arts and the Intellect; Video Games and Learning; International Education; The Pedagogy of Poverty; Patriotism and Education; Improving Low-Performing Schools. How might these themes play out in school conversations about teaching and learning strategies? In proposals to revise the curriculum?
- Perform a similar trend watch for music periodicals for practitioners and researchers such as the *Music Educators Journal; Teaching Music; The Instrumentalist; Choral Journal; American String Teacher; General Music Today; Update: Applications of Research in Music Education; Jazz Educators Journal; Journal of Research in Music Education;* the *Bulletin of the Council for Research in Music Education;* and others.

How does calling a new idea a "trend" influence how teachers respond to the idea? You may wish to converse with teachers in the field to find out what they think of current initiatives and how they have been introduced and implemented in their schools.

Trends and reform initiatives undoubtedly have impact on music teachers' classrooms and programs. When sufficient momentum builds, you can begin to notice how any particular idea starts to surface in publications, conference presentations, school inservice meetings, and in the conversations of teachers. As we have stated, music teachers exercise their professional judgment by deciding whether to implement these ideas into their classrooms, and weighing whether any given new idea forwards their overall goals for music learning. They also make conscious decisions about developing and promoting the idea to others. We will return shortly to this concept of change agentry within the music curriculum, but first, we invite you to imagine a school setting that is most likely different from any school in your experience. We describe an imaginary high school where, in contrast to a small percentage of students who elect music study, nearly 90% of the students at this school are enrolled. You will see why as you read on . . .

INTERLUDE 5.1
Welcome to Musictopia High School

You realize that something about this high school is unusual from the moment you pass through the intricately carved bronze doors into the light-filled central atrium of the music suite. Immediately, you notice an intricate mix of sounds emanating from rehearsal spaces and classrooms located around the central atrium. As you circle the space, stopping outside each door to listen, you hear a group singing the songs of South African Township choirs; a fine wind ensemble playing with artistry and precision; a jazz combo performing intricate polyrhythms; and energetic sounds from the music lab, where small groups of students are clustered around keyboards, drum sets, and guitars, trying out various solutions for covering popular tunes. Peering through the window of one well-appointed classroom, you see students giving multimedia presentations— this one appears to be focused on the music of China. The students are displaying slides of the pipa, zheng, and erhu as they play recordings of the instruments. You notice the central hub of activity in this beautifully appointed wing of the building—labeled the Music Help Desk. Several students are seated at computer monitors as peer tutors help them enter notation for music they have recently composed. The scores for several compositions are framed next to the photographs of their creators and photographs of recent performances of the works. An animated discussion in the Audio Library draws your attention, where students are debating which composers, works, songs and photographs should be included in a presentation on Innovative Musical Ideas at the Turn of the 21st Century for a social studies class.

A bulletin board nearby lists the class offerings for the quarter, which include Concert Choir, Madrigal Singers, Voices of the World Choir, Concert Band, Wind Ensemble, Chamber Orchestra, Musictopia Symphony, as well as classes in Songwriting, Composing for Film, Popular Music and Popular Culture, Musics of the World's Cultures, Jazz Improvisation, and several intriguing categories under Small Ensembles including Javanese Gamelan, Reggae, Turntabling, and something called "Electronic Melange." There are also sign-up sheets for lessons in a wide variety of instruments and vocal classifications for beginning, intermediate, and advanced students. Apparently, students can branch out to learn multiple instruments if they so choose; the music department's schedule extends into the late afternoon to accommodate flexible interests. To your astonishment, you count that there are twelve music teachers listed, each with a variety of specialties. The bulletin board also lists upcoming concerts, guest lectures, events and trips into the community, including the sign-up sheet for an upcoming Musical Showcase, which several students have already filled in with the names of performers in their small groups, and the titles of the pieces they plan to perform. It appears that not only do students eagerly enroll for the courses in this appetizing menu of electives; they also develop leadership by offering lessons to other students in areas of their interest.

Can you envision your own version of Musictopia High School, Middle School, or Elementary School? Where does such a school exist and where can you find an application to teach there?

The Contexts of Change and Teacher Agency

The Musictopia scenario represents a vision of a school that in many ways extends and diversifies current images of school music programs. Although such a music department may not exist (or perhaps it does), this imaginary description prepares you to think about how schools and music programs might be substantially different from what they are at the present. When you think deeply about the gap between what you envision as *possible* in education, and what you know to be more typically the case, or normative, challenging questions follow. Who holds the power to initiate widespread reform in education or music education? Where is this power located? How are teachers' decisions affected by the intentions and plans of individuals, groups, and forces outside of the classroom? Decker Walker (2003) created this complicated but illuminating diagram (Figure 5.5) to represent the American curriculum influence system.

Unlike Great Britain, for example, where teachers are expected to follow a national curriculum scheme, schools in the US are influenced by "a distributed system of decision-making loosely organized into overlapping and contending networks of authority and influence that operate in a strong national context of ideas and institutions" (Walker, 2003, p. 102). Try tracing the source of some recent curricular ideas through this complicated diagram (for example, Arnold Schwarzenegger, who is both a celebrity and a state governor, has used his influence to promote physical education in schools, both from a national platform and in California). Who might need to be convinced of curricular breadth and flexibility in order to support a music program like the one described for Musictopia High School?

Another way to think about curricular change and influence is to consider how different stakeholders and participants in education may have different views of what is important that exist concurrently with other views. Bresler analyzed how the concept of "school music" is shaped and defined in three contexts—micro, meso, and macro (Bresler, 1998). She studied the operational curriculum from the perspective of teachers' beliefs and practices in the classroom (the "micro" context), the structures and goals of the school system (the "meso" context), and more generalized policies, systems, and cultural values that influence the curriculum (the "macro" context). Bresler demonstrated how these realms are interrelated. The decentralized system of education in the US, for example (macro level), allows for considerable teacher autonomy and idiosyncrasy (micro level). Expectations for school music that are reflected in a school's mission or attitude toward the arts (meso level) may influence how a music teacher organizes the music program (micro level). Bresler observes that "the mutual shaping of contexts . . .

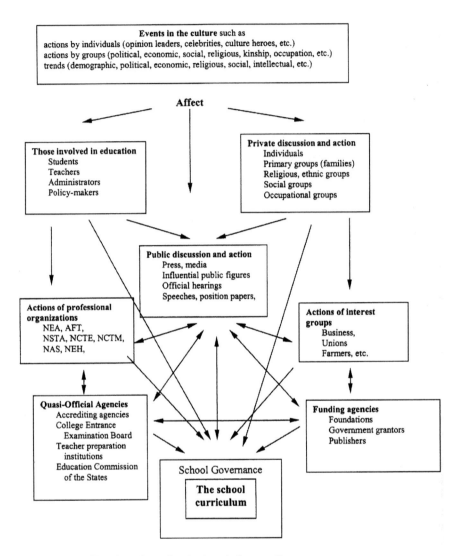

FIGURE 5.5. The American Curriculum Influence System.
Walker, D. F. (2003). *Fundamentals of curriculum: Passion and professionalism* (2nd ed.). Mahwah, NJ: Lawrence Erlbaum. Reprinted with permission from Lawrence Erlbaum, Associates, 2003, all rights reserved.

creates the genre of school music" (p. 2). These insights help us understand how music teachers operate in a climate of freedom that is simultaneously tempered by expectations, policies, and societal norms.

The "micro" context may be the most productive place to begin in thinking about what teachers can imagine, develop, and implement in the music classroom. Returning to Mary Kennedy's study, *Inside Teaching*, again, we learned that in her study of classroom teachers, she observed that they have considerable leeway in making decisions within their classrooms about curriculum content, the sequence of instruction, and the interplay of time, ideas, and people that make up the fabric of classrooms. Kennedy observed:

> Teachers [in the United States] have remarkable flexibility in what they teach and how they teach it. Virtually all other countries have national curricula, which can significantly influence practice. For example, in a comparison of American, Chinese, and Japanese schools, Stevenson and Stigler (1992) found that in the Asian schools, which had national curricula and prescribed texts, the lessons in all classrooms were virtually the same from one day to the next. And while American teachers are all provided with textbooks and other materials, they can and do skip sections they think are irrelevant and add material not covered by the text (Porter et al., 1989).

> Teachers also design their own classroom settings, including what is on the walls, how the furniture is arranged, whether student activities are structured or unstructured, and whether students work alone or in groups. They often create their own demonstrations, their own problems for students, their own homework assignments. (Kennedy, 2005, p. 3)

You may find yourself thinking that Kennedy's description of textbooks, required materials, and other aspects of classroom life does not apply in the same way to music settings. Understanding the contexts of change for music teachers, and the degree to which they can innovate and change their practices may involve some additional reflection.

TAKE ACTION 5.5
Flexibility and Music Teachers

Write several paragraphs to elaborate on this idea: *Music teachers in the United States have remarkable flexibility in what they teach and how they teach it.* Can you give some specific examples of the kind of flexibility music teachers enjoy? By what evidence can you make these claims? How could you confirm your claims about teacher flexibility?

Is this flexibility the same for teachers of other subjects? Why or why not?

The Reform-Minded Music Teacher

Thiessen and Barrett (2002) have described how teachers enact changes in their classrooms that stem from their desires to enhance the learning experiences of students within music classrooms and across the school as part of more general reform efforts. They describe such teachers as exhibiting *reform-mindedness*, a "deeply ingrained and habitual dedication to improvement on the part of teachers" (Thiessen & Barrett, p. 762). Describing how music teachers participate in school-wide reform initiatives is complicated, particularly since many comprehensive school reform models focus on student achievement in subjects such as math and reading, while making little mention of students' experiences in the arts or music specifically. In this case, music teachers may find themselves in a curious and perhaps difficult position as they attempt to support the overall goals of the school settings in which they teach while also acting as strong advocates for the importance of music and the other arts in students' school experiences. Thiessen and Barrett used a musical metaphor to suggest how such teachers adapt features of general reform models to suit the particular characteristics of music learning, or create variants of the ideas that suit musical contexts. "Reform-minded music teachers function in the same way as good musical arrangers, extracting the prominent themes and motives of the reform initiative to create a new setting of the ideas, one that fits the available resources of the school and the particularities of the students and teachers involved in the change" (Thiessen & Barrett, p. 775).

The Emotional Dimensions of Change in Teaching

As you recall from Chapters 2 and 3, the process of learning to teach and the life cycles of teachers are infused with emotion and a sense of personal responsibility. You will recall that both Berliner's and Fessler's descriptions of teachers' work and career pathways drew upon this central aspect of teachers' lives. Andy Hargreaves has studied school reform, educational change processes, the culture of teaching, and most recently, the emotional dimensions of change in teaching. Although it is not often mentioned in the literature on educational change, teachers' emotional landscapes are crucial in understanding both the satisfactions and frustrations of altering one's practice. Hargreaves argues convincingly for paying attention to teachers' feelings, aspirations, and deeply felt personal investments in their work:

> Good teaching is charged with positive emotion. It is not just a matter of knowing one's subject, being efficient, having the correct competencies, or learning all the right techniques. Good teachers are not just well-oiled machines. They

are emotional, passionate beings who connect with their students and fill their work and their classes with pleasure, creativity, challenge, and joy. (Hargreaves, 1998, p. 835)

Hargreaves interviewed a group of 32 innovative Canadian middle school teachers who demonstrated a reform-minded approach to their work. He found four prominent themes in his study:
1. that teachers expressed strong desires to forge strong emotional and social bonds with students, and put a premium on establishing these interpersonal relationships;
2. that open-ended schedules with longer time blocks (which was part of the reform) permitted them to respond more flexibly to student needs in cognitive, social, and emotional realms;
3. that they drew upon a wide variety of teaching strategies, which they found creatively challenging and satisfying, and that made teaching exciting and satisfying; and
4. that teachers planned their curricula based on their knowledge of student interests, and experienced a sense of play and improvisation as they developed learning activities for the students. For these teachers, the emotional currents of teaching were fundamental to the way they embraced change proposals and made them meaningful and fulfilling to students.

It should be no surprise that the emotional dimensions of teaching are often prominent in the conversations and interactions of music teachers, as they implement changes that will benefit students in their programs, while at the same time supporting the overall goals and mission of the school in which they teach. One such teacher is described in Barrett (2005). Nick White, a high school instrumental music teacher, describes how he reorganized his classroom so that students would develop musical independence through participating in chamber groups and musical creativity through composing with the aid of technology. In an interview, Nick explained how he set aside two days per week of his band rehearsal to allow students to form chamber music groups in which they took more responsibility for rehearsing and preparing repertoire. He also implemented a mini-class in music technology, "Imagination Station," to encourage students to create their own pieces. In reconfiguring the traditional band rehearsal from five days a week to three, Nick took considerable risks that the overall performance quality of his ensemble might suffer. In contrast, he found that the musical capabilities of his students were enhanced because they became more self-directed and invested in their musical growth. Nick's emotional investment in this project revealed his willingness to disrupt typical patterns of ensemble settings because he felt strongly that this would foster musical growth among his students.

TAKE ACTION 5.6
Change Story Interview

Using Nick White's story as an example (Barrett, 2005), find a music teacher in the field who has either implemented changes in the curriculum by adapting and responding to an initiative from the "outside" (such as a requirement set in place by the school) or from the "inside" (a change project that the music teacher has implemented on her/his own initiative). Develop questions to include in your interview protocol. Interview that person and write up a brief summary of what you learn. If you can find a teacher who is working on a project that is related to your interests and teaching area, this will be most advantageous. Summarize the teacher's ideas about curricular change and reflect on the ways that this interview prepares you to initiate or respond to changes in teaching.

TAKE ACTION 5.7
Critical Incident Interview

Hargreaves' work on the emotional dimensions of change in teaching is also a fruitful area for interviews (Hargreaves, 2005). In a series of interviews with 50 elementary and secondary teachers of varying ages in Canada, he focused on critical incidents in their teaching, defined as "vivid moments and experiences of positive and negative emotions in relation to interaction with colleagues, students, parents and administrators" (p. 969). These incidents "reveal, like a flashbulb, the major choice and change times in people's lives" (p. 970). In planning the methodology for the study, Hargreaves reasoned that this focus on critical incidents "pushes people past vague euphemisms and bland generalities, embedding their recollections in the gritty details of significant experience" (p. 970).

Although this might seem like a risky approach because it encourages teachers to speak openly about their deep-seated concerns and dilemmas, consider developing some interview questions that will evoke these pivotal occasions for teachers to confront their feelings about their work. You might ask teachers to recall occasions of particular satisfaction and accomplishment, times of doubt and discouragement, events that marked a turning point in their attitudes toward teaching, or ways that they sustain their emotional energies to meet the needs of students in the face of challenges they encounter on a daily basis.

What follows is the report of an interview conducted by one student, Ted, of an urban instrumental music teacher, Kate, and her particular change story. In this interview, Kate describes her early years of teaching instrumental music in an urban setting.

AT CLOSE RANGE 5.1
Curricular Change through Caring Relationships: Kate's Story as Told by Ted

The words "curricular change" strike a chord of apprehension in the hearts and minds of many instrumental music educators. Music educators, often overworked and underpaid, are afraid that any phrase that has a form of the word "curriculum" in it is inherently a call for more paperwork that will eat up more of their most valuable and unfortunately most scarce resource—time. Kate Fitzpatrick, who took a job at a middle-class school in the Columbus City School District right after graduating from college, is a perfect example that curricular change does not have to bring with it an increased load of paperwork. During her four years at Columbus Northland High School, Kate revitalized the instrumental music program as changes grew naturally out of her desire to fulfill community expectations and allow students the room to study music of their own choosing.

Before Kate's arrival, Northland's instrumental music program had a longstanding tradition of excellence. In a school that was struggling academically and that faced increasing problems of racial tension, especially between the Somalian minority and the African-American majority, the marching band was the pride of the school and the surrounding community. Columbus Northland was the only high school out of 14 in the district that had managed to keep its instrumental music program going strong throughout the years. Thus, the band was a focal point of the school and community's identity. Strong traditions were closely guarded, and were as specific as the close marching style of the marching band. They were also as general as the expectation of a superior rating for the concert band every year.

Kate was almost surprised when she was hired right out of college to be the new band director at Northland. She knew that she would face many obstacles. Not only was she the youngest person ever to hold the job; she was also the first female director. While Kate did not have previous experience in an urban environment, she was not afraid of learning. She had applied for the job based on the quality of the program alone. In her first year, Kate found her students very leery about trusting and accepting her. The parents were adamant about holding onto traditions. During this time, Kate worked hard at building relationships and calming fears that she planned to make big changes to the program.

Part of what helped Kate connect with students was her honesty. She told her students that she would like to know more about the music they listened to. Students began to bring in music for her to hear. Gradually, the students felt the music they listened to was valued by Kate. In this racially mixed high school (approximately 70% black and 30% mixed White and Hispanic), Kate was especially attentive to racial issues. In her interview, she told me that she tried to reflect the following attitude: "I'm not the white teacher pretending she's black, trying to pretend I'm a part of your culture, that I know anything about what you are going through." In the spirit of sharing, Kate brought in music from her own Irish background on St. Patrick's Day for students to listen to. Other students then felt comfortable sharing about their own cultures, and Kate specifically remembers when Nigerian students brought in music and food from their country to share with the class.

Kate's attitude of, "I'm not from your culture, so you have to teach me about it," led directly into students asking whether they could play "their music" in marching band. Of course, recognizing the disconnect between the popular music and "art music," Kate told them that they could go ahead and arrange something. Students downloaded and used the free version of Finale's notepad and set to work arranging their favorite pop tunes. Kate later added a rule that they had to play the original version of the song for her before she gave it her approval because of one incident at a football game where the entire student body started singing along with an inappropriately profane rap song that the band was playing. Nonetheless, this attention to popular culture sparked students' interest.

Some students who got their start arranging songs for the marching band then moved on to actually compose pieces for concert band. Reflecting on her experience, Kate believes that she could have done more with encouraging arranging and composition, especially during concert band season. However, Kate recognizes that with more students arranging and composing, she would have been confronted with the issue of how much "standard" concert band repertoire to play and how much "new music" that her students composed. In any case, one of Kate's outstanding student composers went on to Ohio State and is currently completing his last year with a double major in music education and composition.

Interestingly, Kate found that when she did a Motown show, her African-American students did not necessarily connect to the music in any significant way; Motown is the kind of music their parents listened to and is not necessarily a part of their identity. Similarly, jazz held little cultural significance to her African-American students; Kate said that having her students play jazz was akin to having them play Mozart. It was simply not a part of their identities. Music that students did strongly identify with was more recent; for example, music from the movie Drumline *was hugely popular on the marching field.*

Music educators would do well to learn from Kate's example that curricular change is best accomplished slowly, over time. Kate did not go in with an idea about what the best curriculum was for her students. Instead, she learned from them and began to tailor the program to suit their needs as well as the needs of the community and school administration. By making her curriculum, and repertoire especially, more relevant to her students, it seems that Kate was able to lead her students toward deeper levels of musical understanding.

Another student need that came to Kate's attention was a way for high school students with no prior musical training to play in the band. Many immigrant students came to Kate and asked if they could become part of the band, and, unfortunately, Kate had to turn away many of these students in her first year as a teacher. Especially in a community where the marching band was a unifying factor, turning these students away kept them at an arm's length from feeling like they were a part of their new community. So, Kate asked the administration to start a beginning high school band, and here students could learn an instrument for a year. After one year of beginning band, students could be in the second concert band, and many of them were able to make great improvements in their playing throughout their high school careers.

As Kate recounted her experiences at Columbus Northland, she was surprised to discover the many innovations that had happened in the music program as a result of her teaching. She never felt that she was purposely trying to change things; rather, she was responding to students and guiding them forward in their learning about music. Kate feels quite strongly that the changes she made to the curriculum at Northland came out of her relationships with her students. Viewed from this perspective, curricular change is not the mountain of paperwork imagined by many music educators. Rather, curricular change is a regular part of the teaching process of any self-reflective, caring teacher.

Change and the Moral Dimensions of Teaching

In closing, it is important to return to the notion of teaching as a moral act, one in which teachers and other school personnel strive to provide fulfilling educational experiences for students, but also look broadly to the power of education in transforming society. By acting in ways that are informed by deep conviction, teachers' work is guided by ethical, moral, and often political beliefs. Dewey wrote of these larger purposes in stating, "what the best and wisest parent wants for his own child, that must the community want for all its children. Any other ideal for our schools is narrow and unlovely; acted upon, it destroys our democracy" (in Archambault, 1964, p. 295). The art educator Elliot Eisner, himself a proponent of Dewey's ideals, forwards the metaphor that schools are cultures, both in the anthropological sense of shared values, practices, and beliefs, and also in a biological sense as a medium for growing minds. He writes, "how schools are organized, what is taught in them, the kinds of norms they embrace, and the relationships they foster among adults and children all matter, for they shape the experiences that students are likely to have and in the process influence who children will become" (Eisner, 2002, p. 3). When you consider the potential impact that teachers have in contributing to this capacious view of growth, any proposal for change takes on greater significance. Mike Rose, who journeyed across the United States for four years visiting classrooms in rural, urban, and suburban communities, sought to find classrooms where teachers created vibrant classroom communities, inspired by their desire to make positive changes for their students. In his book, *Possible Lives,* he wrote that a defining attribute of good teaching is the "tendency to push on the existing order of things" (1995, p. 428), propelled by visions of what students might become.

Within music education, reflection on aims and purposes is ongoing and essential. Jorgensen makes a compelling case for taking a broad view of music education's purpose and for looking to music to represent and encapsulate broader societal themes: "Music education provides a window into what happens in education generally. It also can be an agent for change not only in education but also in the wider society. The arts are important ingredients of cultural life, and education fundamentally involves the transmission and transformation of culture" (Jorgensen, 2003, p. xiii). She challenges music teachers to think beyond the practical and technical demands of teaching to seek "greater humanity, civility, justice and freedom" (p. 12) for all students. To bring about the kinds of transformation Jorgensen sees as possible for our profession, she seeks the kind of teachers who are:

> Dedicated and knowledgeable musicians; understand their personal strengths and weaknesses; and have a clear vision of what they seek to accomplish, high expectations of themselves and others tempered with compassion and realism, a love of the musics of which they are exponents and of the particular people, young or old, whom they instruct, and a desire to communicate their knowledge to their students and to improve the musical traditions of which they are heirs. To accomplish this requires people of integrity who are bright, articulate, tactful, compassionate, and astute, the best musicians and communicators, the very cream of society. (p. 131)

Woodford (2005) challenges teacher education programs to develop "idealistic and visionary music teachers who see themselves as public intellectuals and democratic leaders of children . . . charged with creatively meeting the needs of all of society and not just the rich and elite among us" (p. 99). For teachers new to the field, Jorgensen's or Woodford's charges may seem daunting, but to return to the Havel poem at the beginning of this chapter, we are reminded that "Whether all is really lost / or not depends entirely on / whether or not I am lost." In other words, the way that your decisions and beliefs about teaching or learning influence what you do on a daily basis reflects the kind of moral compass you use to guide your work. The way you define your work in music education as the primary vehicle for realizing aims such as expressive performance, the development of musical independence, the education of feeling, lifelong engagement in music, and social justice should guide how you initiate and respond to change.

In this chapter, you have been encouraged to consider how change is a constant theme in teaching. As you seek to understand the oscillating tensions between tradition and innovation in music education, learn to articulate and challenge worn patterns in need of fresh thinking, observe how teachers are often asked to change their classroom practices, and become more knowledgeable about current reform proposals, you will also develop your capacities as a reform-minded music teacher. Becoming strategically aware of the various influences that motivate change, and of the emotional commitment and moral purpose of teachers who initiate change on behalf of their students, will suit you well for a lifetime of growth and satisfaction in music teaching.

In the remainder of this book, you will continue to develop your skills, dispositions, and understanding by engaging in further study of yourself as a teacher; of students, colleagues, administrators, parents, and others you will encounter; of school contexts, and of curricular matters that attend music teaching and learning.

For Your Inquiry

Bartel, L. R. (Ed.). (2004). *Questioning the music education paradigm*. **Waterloo, Canada: Canadian Music Educators' Association.**

This is a provocative collection of essays that challenge the status quo in music education, and encourage teachers to define more clearly what we mean when we refer to "music education" in general. Authors address challenging topics such as learning environments in music classrooms, inclusion, gender, competition, popular music and intolerance, and even a comparison of the assumptions that guide sports programs and music programs.

Fullan, M. (2007). *The new meaning of educational change* **(4th ed.). New York, NY: Teachers College Press.**

Michael Fullan is a noted scholar who has studied school reform and educational change for several decades. In *The New Meaning of Educational Change*, he synthesizes the extensive and sometimes daunting literature on change in schools. Of particular interest are two chapters. Chapter 7, which focuses on teachers' experiences of change, begins with this profound statement: "Educational change depends on what teachers do and think—it's as simple and as complex as that" (p. 129). In chapter 14, Fullan describes the conditions and supports necessary for teachers to sustain their own intellectual development while meeting the pressing demands of classroom life. He emphasizes that teachers should be learning every day, continuously improving their capabilities and understandings. Reading this book will lead you to realize how the forces outside of schools that attempt to improve what happens within them often fail to account for teachers' roles in bringing about meaningful changes in education.

Hargreaves, A. (1994). *Changing teachers, changing times: Teachers' work and culture in the postmodern age.* **New York, NY: Teachers College Press.**

In this challenging and insightful book, Andy Hargreaves describes the culture of teaching and draws upon research that explains how teachers negotiate many competing demands for their time and expertise. Of particular interest is Hargreaves' work on contrived collegiality, in which teachers are asked to work on projects and to collaborate with other teachers in response to mandates rather than self-generated initiatives. He uses the metaphor of a "moving mosaic" to illustrate how change occurs in dynamic, interdependent learning organizations.

Jorgensen, E. R. (2003). *Transforming music education*. Bloomington, IN: Indiana University Press.

Estelle Jorgensen draws from many different sources to inform five essays for transforming education and music education. She challenges teachers to think beyond overly simplistic dichotomies of "either this or that" to examine ideas in a dialogical fashion that encourages change by contemplating multiple alternatives. In this dialogical view, ideas about music education are examined through considering the advantages and disadvantages of each, leading to a richer and more complex synthesis of possible alternatives.

Rose, M. (1995). *Possible lives: The promise of public education in America*. New York, NY: Penguin Books.

Although not specifically about change, Mike Rose gives us richly detailed portraits of teachers and schools in diverse communities across America—from large urban districts such as Los Angeles, Chicago, and New York to smaller communities in Montana, Kentucky, and Mississippi. These cases of practice show how teachers live out principles of democratic education in the everyday contexts of classrooms, often drawing our attention to extraordinary individuals who provide a vibrant and liberating educational experience for students. This book provides an uplifting antidote to bleak criticisms of public education.

six
Methodologies for Exploring Teaching and Learning

We all carry worlds in our heads, and those worlds are decidedly different. We educators set out to teach, but how can we reach the worlds of others when we don't even know they exist? Indeed, many of us don't even realize that our own worlds exist only in our heads and in the cultural institutions we have built to support them.
Lisa Delpit, *Other People's Children*, 1995, p. xiv

The chief subject matter of school, viewed culturally, is school itself. That is how most students experience it, and it determines what meaning they make of it.
Jerome Bruner, *Culture of Education*, 1996, p. 28

Our classrooms ought to be nurturing and thoughtful and just all at once; they ought to pulsate with multiple conceptions of what it means to be human and alive. . . . We must want our students to achieve friendship as each one stirs to wide-awakeness, to imaginative action, and to renewed consciousness of possibility.
Maxine Greene, *Releasing the Imagination*, 1995, p. 43

FOCUS
This chapter presents a set of integrated, yet distinct methodologies for exploring self and context in relation to teaching and learning. Where chapters 1–5 provide

primarily theoretical bases for a personal orientation to teacher education with introductory exercises, illustrative narratives and supportive research, this chapter extends and refines those exercises and understandings through in-depth reflection and writing. A central idea in this chapter is that teacher learning is significantly informed by practices and methodologies of self and community inquiry. A major goal is acquiring the disposition to engage in systematic and persistent investigation into your own teaching and professional environments in order to address problems of practice and avenues of change.

Studying Curriculum: Commonplaces

In the late 20th century, Joseph Schwab revolutionized the field of curriculum by forwarding the idea that curriculum work (including things like instruction, organization, selection of experiences, assessment, policy) should be rooted in practical inquiry by those directly involved in teaching and learning. From his perspective, Schwab imagined teachers to be curious and inquisitive individuals concerned about their own practices and the complexities and subtleties of their effects (1959/1978), not necessarily individuals trained to be technicians charged with delivering pre-packaged materials and skill work to groups of learners. Schwab considered teachers to be *curriculum makers* and *curriculum inquirers.* Furthermore, Schwab believed that inquiry into any education situation could be understood in terms of "four commonplaces": learners, teachers, subject matter and milieu (or context) (Schwab, 1983).

Schwab's image of teachers also included the notion that teachers possess a great deal of knowledge about their own work. He believed teachers to be the "fountainhead[s] of curricular decisions," and that no deliberations could be complete without their active involvement. Teachers, he stated are the "agents of education" (1954/1978), and not objects to be manipulated by outside agents. The idea that teachers are both curriculum inquirers and makers *and* sources of knowledge about their teaching has been taken up by the contemporary idea that to be a teacher is to be "a student of teaching" rather than a person who instructs students in lessons about something (Bullough & Gitlin, 2001).

William Schubert (1986) has characterized Schwab's commonplaces as a powerful heuristic (conceptual and analytical device) for inquiring about how each commonplace might interact with another and how each commonplace might interact as a whole. For example, How might a student clique in a classroom affect the way a teacher designs a lesson? (This question focuses on the interactions between students and teachers.) Or, How might the way a method book presents a concept or skill in a particular subject influence the way a student understands the concept or skill? (This question focuses on the interactions between subject matter and students.) Such questions allow teachers multiple entry points and multiple pathways to pursue in their deliberations about curriculum matters. Plus, it allows inquiry to be more relevant to particular situations.

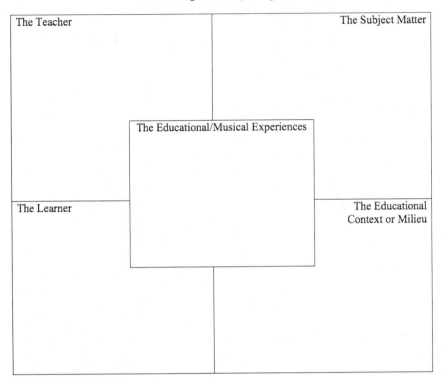

FIGURE 6.1. Embedded Squares Diagram

In music education, Schwab's commonplaces have been used as a heuristic for understanding teacher learning (Barrett & Rasmussen, 1996; Campbell, 1999; Miranda, Robbins, & Stauffer, 2007; Olson, Barrett, Rasmussen, Barresi, & Jensen, 2000). Figure 6.1, the "Embedded Squares," is taken from Barrett and Rasmussen's work with preservice teachers. The diagram was created as a space to collect thoughts about any one of the commonplaces, or any interaction between commonplaces that a person might observe when in a school or watching a video of teaching, or even a movie about teaching. The diagram can also be used to generate questions for inquiry (Take Action 6.1).

At the center of the embedded squares in Figure 6.1 is "Educational/Musical Experiences." The central block is the "nexus" among the four commonplaces because it draws attention to core curriculum concerns related to quality. After we have observed, we often summarize by evaluating the overall impact or quality of this educational/musical experience for the participants. What distinguishes casual opinion from informed judgment are the *criteria* that are used when perceptive observations are considered in light of the principles and values held by the observer. Recall that Schwab states that many criteria are necessary for curriculum inquiry.

TAKE ACTION 6.1
Curriculum Inquiry: Observing with the Commonplaces in Mind

Read the following quote taken from one of Joseph Schwab's papers focused on curriculum inquiry:

> Only as the teacher uses the classroom as the occasion and the means to reflect upon education as a whole . . . as a laboratory in which to translate reflections into actions and thus to test reflections, actions and outcomes, against many criteria is he [sic] a good . . . teacher. (1959/1978, pp. 182–183)

In their own experiences as students, most preservice teachers have spent countless hours in classrooms observing what teachers do and say. Observing with Schwab's framework in mind is helpful because thinking about the commonplaces prompts you to shift your attention from the teacher to the students, the content or subject matter of the lesson, and the aspects of the educational context that influence what is learned and taught. Some general recommendations to guide looking in on music learning and teaching include:

- Seek first to describe, and be cautious about jumping to conclusions that lead you too quickly to broad generalizations or hastily formed opinions.
- Strive for nuance and fine discrimination in order to achieve meaningful distinctions in your descriptions.
- Be discerning in what you record by distinguishing the trivial from the significant.
- Consider the purposes of your observation. What do you hope to gain from viewing and reflecting on this lesson or rehearsal?

Below are a few commonplace questions to prompt your thinking about "life in the classroom." After you have generated your questions, spend some time in various classrooms recording what you see. As you begin to shift your attention, spend time on refining your observational skills, keeping in mind some of the guidelines suggested above.

Questions related to the Teacher

How does the teacher sequence learning?
How does the teacher respond to students?
What instructional moves does the teacher make?
In what ways does the teacher serve as a musical model for students?

Questions related to the Learner

What do the students do and say throughout the lesson or rehearsal?
How are the students engaged and how do you know?
In what diverse ways are students interacting with music?
What evidence of students' prior knowledge can you discern?
What individual differences seem apparent (or might remain hidden)?
How do learners interact with one another as well as with the teacher?

Questions related to the Subject Matter

What musical elements or musical problems are the focus of the lesson or rehearsal?
How do the materials used portray music? For example: Are musical examples presented as musical wholes or as smaller segments? Is music communicated through sound? Musical symbols? Some other form of representation? Is the music being made by the teachers and students or is a recording the sound source?
What styles of music are used, more or less frequently?
Are there instances when the teacher or students focus on content that is not directly related to music (subjects outside of music, social/emotional learning, etc.)?

Questions related to the Milieu or Educational Context

How is the room arranged? How does this arrangement support or inhibit learning?
What values are portrayed in the classroom through posters, other materials?
What evidence of the school community or culture can you observe (such as school rules, traditions, and expectations; collaborations between students, teachers, parents, and administrators; or challenges and opportunities faced by the school)?
How does the setting of the school (rural, urban, suburban) influence what is learned or taught?

Repeat this Take Action often. Work with another colleague or in a small study group. Compare observations and descriptions. Generate new sets of questions. Video-record your own teaching, and then do a self-analysis or have a group of colleagues watch and analyze your teaching with you.

Criteria are judgments on the qualities of individual things, ideas, and actions. The function of criteria, as Eisner points out, is to deepen experience with something particular not necessarily to make comparisons about things in general

(2002). According to Dewey, criteria promote inquiry (Dewey, 1934) because they require us to look and think more carefully. Educational and musical experiences are likely to be most powerful and moving when teachers have a set of criteria to use as a framework for analyzing and assessing their work and interactions with others.

Criteria and Quality of Educational/Musical Experiences

Whether you are focused on instructional issues, curriculum concerns, students and their engagements, or evaluating learning, teachers are always exercising judgment and making decisions. Although teachers use a variety of sources to help them make informed decisions—their personal belief systems, mentors and more knowledgeable others, published materials and guidelines, student interest—most teachers rely upon criteria. Sometimes criteria are quite explicit, like the standards used to measure the accuracy of pitch production. Sometimes the criteria are more implicit, like the impressions created when we say a performance was very "musical" or quite expressive. In both instances, criteria help teachers make judgments about effectiveness, and aid them in planning and making decisions.

In judging the quality of a piece of music, Reimer (1991), for example, suggests that we can base our assessment of its worth on:

1. craftsmanship, the expertness by which the materials of art are molded into expressiveness;
2. sensitivity, "the depth and quantity of feeling captured in the dynamic form of the work";
3. imagination, the "vividness of an art object and its performance"; and
4. authenticity, the "genuineness of the artist's interaction with . . . materials in which the control . . . includes a giving way to the demands of the material" (pp. 132–136).

Reimer's framework is helpful in making decisions about the pieces of music we might select for study. It is also helpful in teaching students how to evaluate the different qualities of the various pieces they download and listen to, create, and perform.

In education, John Dewey (1938) suggests that educational experiences are likely to be worthwhile if they are: (a) democratic in structure—including teaching-learning relationships that are communal and self-governing in their organization; and (b) built on "continuity and interaction" or active engagement. *Continuity*, as described by Dewey, is the idea that children learn best when they connect past and present experiences, both in and out of school. This connection helps create new knowledge and provides opportunities for future growth. Today we might call this "learning from prior knowledge." *Interaction* refers to the relationship between a psychology of the child (needs and interests) and the logic of a particular subject matter (its organization, principles, rules, vocabulary). Teaching that bridges the gap between these two frameworks of understanding is often referred to as interest-based or exploratory learning within a subject matter. A third criterion that is at the heart of worthwhile educational experiences is the idea of problem-based or inquiry-based learning. This kind of learning is best characterized as the teacher and the child exploring together problems of interest within the logic of a subject. Today we might call this common zone of inquiry as guided discovery or teacher facilitated learning. The key criterion that acts as glue between the social and individual aspects of learning is the idea that learning be a regenerative or a never-ending process. For Dewey, a worthwhile educational experience has immediate effect on the child's interests and lays a foundation that allows an individual to contribute positively to society. Non-educative experiences have little or no lasting effects.

Maxine Greene's (1995, 2001) thoughts on artistic expression provide another lens for looking at and judging the quality of arts experiences that we provide in schools. Greene suggest that arts experiences are: (a) fundamentally subjective, individuals are centers of choice and evaluation—in other words, the "personal" matters; (b) driven by imagination and perception in order "to awaken; to disclose the unseen and unexpected" (1995, p. 28); and (c) multi-perspectival, because arts are situated in diverse contexts, generate diversity of thought and respect inclusiveness. Although not strictly stated as criteria, Greene's thoughts clearly point to fundamental qualities of artistic encounters that can inform teachers' decision making in curriculum matters.

TAKE ACTION 6.2
The Criteria of Scholars—And Your Musical Experiences

Combine the criteria suggested by Reimer, Dewey, and Greene into a single list. Think about each criterion and what each one means by comparing and contrasting the similarities and differences among them. How are the criteria alike? How are they different? What do they have in common?

Before you continue reading, review or take time to complete Take Action 1.2 in Chapter 1 (*Connecting to the Past—Powerful Experiences with Music*). In what ways could your personal powerful experiences with music fit any of the criteria provided by Reimer, Dewey, Greene or all three? How might the use of criteria inform your thinking and work as a music teacher and curriculum creator and inquirer?

As each of these scholars' thinking about educational experiences and artistic creation/experiences suggests, having a conceptual framework for thinking about the quality of our curricular and instructional work in music teaching and learning is important. In thinking about your own personal orientation to music teaching and learning, we would like to suggest that you begin to articulate a set of criteria for assessing the quality of educational and musical experiences. Our own thinking on criteria to use for assessing music education experiences can be found in Figure 6.2.

Generativity. *Generativity is the term we use to describe musical and educational experiences that have the ability to produce, originate or generate additional or new experiences. Generative learning is both spiral-like and dynamic. It feeds off itself in ever-expanding ways. Musical and educational experiences that propel learners to want to know more, to seek out new knowledge or develop and refine skills are generative. Learning experiences that "create a need to know" for students can be generative when student interest is taken into consideration or when a musical problem is formulated in such a way that it is compelling enough for students to want to solve it.*

Musical and educational experiences that tend to follow technical or "accumulative" forms—where knowledge is removed from its context and is broken into discrete tasks or concepts and through an additive process is designed to total up to understanding—are rarely generative. These kinds of experiences, along with curricular materials designed for this kind of learning, tend to lead to prescribed teacher behaviors and disconnected learning. Plus they tend to elevate the acquisition of the "bits" over the "whole," making the "bits" seem like knowledge in and of themselves (Bullough, Holt, & Goldstein, 1984). Teaching questions that get to the heart of a discipline are likely to be generative, especially if they are constructed so as to allow for multiple interpretations and responses. Learning projects that sustain student (and teacher) interest over time and that have multiple pathways for exploring content and developing individual skill are generative.

Vibrancy. *Vibrancy refers to educational experiences that resonate with personal meaning and musical significance. Classes where an energy, force or vitality can be seen or felt are vibrant. Where there is an "aliveness" or "livingness" present among students and teachers, vibrancy is likely to be present. Vibrancy is simultaneously a quality of human interaction (student–teacher or student-student interaction) and a quality of the materials and processes teachers use to engage them. Here Reimer's criteria can be helpful in selecting materials. Vibrancy in human interaction, however, is not directly synonymous with enthusiasm, eagerness, or even passion. Rather vibrancy is more a matter of "mindful engagement" with content and processes. Vibrancy in educational experiences is "minds on/hands on," immediate and sustained learning.*

Facts memorized, coupled with pre-determined tasks to be demonstrated or mastered, can rarely be substituted for the vibrancy of the "educated imagination" (Eisner, 1994). *Processes that engage students' imaginations and creativity through the direct manipulation of sound can be quite vibrant, especially if situated within the generative aspects of a need to know and sustainability. Moreover, interactions that develop sensitivities to sound relationships and their expressiveness have the potential to be vibrant when students are asked to focus perception, create or fashion musical products, or develop technique in order to solve musical problems. Particularly important are learning experiences where learners' identities as musical individuals are addressed and cultivated.*

Residue. *Residue is the "stuff" that remains after an experience is over or long gone. Metaphorically, residue can take many forms—from positive memories to hurtful rejection; from self-initiated agency to denial and isolation. Musical and educational experiences that are generative and vibrant are most likely to produce affirming and positive residue. Music education experiences that spark the imagination, attend to music's expressive qualities, and stimulate wonder are likely to resonate with learners and leave positive impressions.*

In contrast, positive and affirming residue is less likely to occur where emphasis has been placed on content delivery, testing cycles designed to account for content acquisition or skill attainment. One way to think about residue in experiences is to reflect on significant events, individuals or situations that were particularly vibrant. What made those experiences vibrant, and how is it that you are able to recall, reflect, and appreciate those experiences today? Dewey says that having "an experience" possesses qualities similar to what we call vibrancy. The long terms effects of having undergone an experience (memories, recall, reminiscences, initiative, appreciation, understanding, savoring, pleasure, etc.) is what we call residue. Recall in Chapter 1 the Musical Circles of Kara, Brett and Don (Take Action 1.2: Connecting to the Past – Powerful Experiences with Music). What memorable moments can you recall from your own educational and musical experiences that have left a mark on you, or produced positive residue?

FIGURE 6.2. Criteria for Assessing Music Education Experiences

Kinds of Curriculum and their Characteristics

When teachers engage in curriculum matters, what is it exactly they are engaging in? What exactly does curriculum mean? And what matters in curriculum matters? The etymology or word origin of curriculum is derived from Latin, meaning the course or track of a chariot race. By extension curriculum is often thought of as a path or course of action. Metaphorically, curriculum can be seen as a journey of learning and growth that is consciously developed. The use of the term curriculum, however, is quite varied, representing many different ideas, conflicting definitions, contrasting conceptions, and opposing assumptions about knowledge, learners and teacher roles. No one definition or description fits the many different forms and kinds of curricula you are likely to encounter in education. Even so, curriculum matters are always concerned with the key questions of education: "What knowledge is most worthwhile?", "Why is it worthwhile?" and "How is it acquired or created?"

Figure 6.3 provides several contrasting and complementary kinds of curriculum that include: general areas or topics of interest and inquiry; activities and examples that illustrate ideas or practices; and characteristic features or attributes, such as beliefs or intentions. Analyze the different kinds of curriculum and their characterizations found in Figure 6.3. After you have spent some time studying these images take a look at the activities and questions in Take Action 6.3.

Documents. *Goals and standards written and endorsed by professional associations, teams of teachers, or policy-making agencies such as state education departments or accrediting agencies. Curriculum guides, national, state, local standards.*

Overall Plan. *Plan of studies, courses, course content and events that mark progression from elementary to high school, often followed by vocational or college programs.*

Planned Activities. *Lesson, unit, or grading period plans (written and enacted) that teachers design or modify from existing sources. Manuals, outlines, handbooks, teacher editions, student textbooks, methods books that organize subject matter by scope (what is to be included/excluded) and sequence (progression or order). Teaching techniques or tips and motivational devices.*

Subject Matter Acquisition. *Major topics, "big ideas," concepts, rules, procedures, ways of working within a particular discipline. General studies, advanced placement, college prep, vocational, honors, remedial.*

Outcomes. *Concrete forms of evidence that point to strengths/weaknesses of a school program, a student's achievement, test scores, public recognition of the work of students, teachers, school or district. Demonstrated proof of attaining an objective, often described in behavioral terms. Specified/pre-determined end product, behavior or way of thinking based upon intended or specified purpose.*

Experiences. *Experiences ("lived undergoings") of students as they interact with materials, ideas, influential adults, more knowledgeable others, and peers to* *acquire or create knowledge, skills and dispositions. Self-monitoring of progress toward growth; problem-solving, discussion, dialogue, debates, projects.*

Tasks and Concepts. *Sets of tasks or skills to be mastered; acquisition and application of rules, sequencing of tasks from simple to complex; analysis of perception, connection of ideas from simple incidence to generalized ideas.*

Cultural Reproduction. *Direct inculcation of specific cultural values, ways of thinking, ways of working, appreciations that seek to maintain status quo within society; sets of concepts, beliefs, assumptions, practices being consciously reproduced among younger members of a group, community of practice or profession; patriotic events and ideas, dominant economic systems, such as socialistic or capitalistic, folkways.*

Cultural Reconstruction. *Ideas, topics, tools, tasks, concepts, plans, activities, experiences that aid in an agenda of values and knowledge creation that guide students to improve society, cultural institution.*

Expectations. *Desires, aims, goals, outlook, opportunities envisioned by any one or all interested individuals in the education process—administrators, parents, taxpayers, students, state agencies, etc.*

FIGURE 6.3. Kinds of Curriculum and their Characteristics

TAKE ACTION 6.3
Curriculum Deliberations

Questions for Reflection and Discussion

Which kinds of curriculum in Figure 6.3 seem customary or common sense to you? Which seem similar, contradictory? What purposes do you think each kind of curriculum seeks to attain? Which kind of curriculum do you feel is most widespread among educators, among music educators, among the community? What assumptions and beliefs about teachers, about students, about knowledge do each portray? What additional information might you need to be able to understand a specific characterization better?

Questions for Analysis and Reflection

Go to your college library and examine the professional journals and periodicals written for music educators. Select one or two articles to read. What kind(s) of curriculum seems embedded in the author's portrayal of ideas, suggestions, examples or illustrations? Review Focus on Research 1.2 (Gods,

Guides, and Gardeners) in Chapter 1. Three root metaphors were used to analyze the thinking of the preservice music teachers in the study: production, growth, and travel. Apply Campbell and Thompson's characterizations of these three metaphors to the ideas contained in the articles you have selected to read. Which one seems to fit best? Why?

Questions for Deliberation and Debate

With a partner or small group, become a proponent of a single curriculum. Indicate what students should know, be able to do in order to thrive as individuals in contemporary American society. Find another set of individuals who are advocates of a curriculum that seems contradictory or incompatible with yours. Form a debate. Articulate your criticism around the ideas, assumptions, intentions, actions and values embedded in your opponents' images. What counterarguments will you use to build your position?

Projects for Further Inquiry

As you can see, curriculum does not exist in a vacuum; it is highly interdependent with many other influences and forces. Curriculum has an "ecology" of its own. That is, curriculum is "continuously created by its interdependence with the forces in which it is embedded" (Schubert, 1986, p. 35). Recall Figure 5.5 in Chapter 5: "The American Curriculum Influence System" and the kinds of forces that have direct influence on curriculum. Consider the following list of influences derived from Decker Walker's (2003) diagram:

- Administrators
- Supervisors, Chairpersons or Coordinators
- Evaluation
- Research
- Level of schooling—preschool, elementary school, middle school, high school, etc.
- Educational psychology—behaviorism, developmental, cognitive, etc.
- Public law and legal statutes—Title IX (Equal Opportunity in Education Act), PL 94–142—(The Education for the Handicapped Act), etc.
- History—past thinking and practices on curriculum
- Instructional methods
- Technology.

Select any one of these areas (or any area from Figure 5.5) and seek out an individual who specializes in it. Prepare a set of questions that focus on how his or her area works to facilitate the process of curriculum development or implementation. Conversely, ask questions about how the area might get in the way or hinder development.

FOCUS ON RESEARCH 6.1
Seeing and Hearing Music Teaching and Learning

Martina L. Miranda, Janet Robbins and Sandra L. Stauffer (2007) were interested in knowing the extent to which ethnographic/portraiture research was effective in helping students in music teacher preparation courses become more sophisticated in their understanding of music teaching/learning processes. Thirty-six students from three different universities participated in the study. Participants were enrolled in a general music methods course, with the researchers teaching the course at their respective universities. A field component accompanied and was integrated into each of the classes.

Schwab's (1954/1978) "Commonplaces of Schooling" was used by all three professor–researchers as a conceptual framework for organizing students' experiences and assignments, as well as for organizing the study's data collection and analysis processes. To represent their work students used portraiture techniques (See for example, Lawrence-Lightfoot & Davis, 1997; Stake, Bresler, & Mabry, 1991). To represent the findings of the study the researchers used emergent themes, i.e., "big ideas" that surfaced as a result of analyzing the data.

Information and opportunities to use a variety of ethnographic methods were presented through the course. Among the methods the students used were:

- Field notes—writing and analyzing, peer critique of notes
- Observational analysis—including live and video-recordings of classrooms
- Participant-observation—leading/teaching experience, with reflection notes
- Focus group conversations—on-site discussions with classroom teachers and university professors
- Portraiture—drawing images of teachers/teaching based on personal memory, use of photo images to capture on-site (classroom) experiences, essays about experiences.

Students' course work (field notes, reflections, observation analysis, portraiture papers), interviews, in-class discussion and reflections were used as data. Analysis of the data indicated that:

- Students "consistently recognized the interconnected nature of the culture of the music classroom and the teachers and children they observed" (p. 10).
- Regardless of the particularities of different field sites or observations,

students' reflections about teachers, students and content tended to focus on four main themes:

- Respect and relationships
- Motivation and management
- Amazement at children's musical capabilities
- Organization and delivery of content.

Miranda, Robbins and Stauffer noted in their analysis that students seemed to go through a process of personal growth and change—pointing out that the college students were more able to appreciate the range and depth of student learning in the elementary classroom. In addition, the researchers found that for some college students there was a shift in self-concept, indicating a potential efficacy at teaching elementary general music.

As a conclusion, the researchers offer several important implications for learning to teach and professional development:

- Ethnographic techniques that help preservice teachers make a distinction between descriptive and interpretive perspectives aid in their abilities to focus on detail and pre-empts a "rush to judgment," thus facilitating more thoughtful critique.
- Reflections that were identified as especially thoughtful contained questions or discussed options and possibilities related to a class event, topic, musical action, or teacher/student action or interaction. These accounts were in comparison to more generalized critiques.
- Multiple observation experiences in combination with the use of multiple lenses, such as the Schwab commonplaces, along with prolonged engagement at the same site help preservice teachers shift from a "self" perspective to an "others" perspective and/or to a "self in context" perspective.

Studying the Commonplace of Subject Matter—Music

Educators from all fields have relied on Schwab's commonplaces as a framework for curriculum deliberation, analysis, observation, and research. As you noticed in the research study by Miranda, Robbins, and Stauffer, the "four corners" of teacher, learners, subject matter, and educational context or milieu overlap and intersect in any given lesson, rehearsal, or educational experience. Imagine that a group of researchers could study the musical substance and quality of an entire program by systematically observing *what* is learned and taught about music over multiple classrooms and years within a particular school district. Think how valuable it would be to compile these observations and represent them in a meaningful form to provide a global or "big picture" perspective on the overall content of the curriculum. What might be important in looking at the music curriculum from the standpoint of an entire course, class, and cumulative impact of music instruction over time? If you could launch such an investigation of an entire music program from early childhood through adolescence, what would you want to know about the music curriculum as a whole? Would you uncover separate "streams" of musical growth by area, such as band, choir, orchestra, general music? Would these streams cross? Program reviews often seek to answer these kinds of ambitious questions.

On an ongoing basis, music teachers design educational experiences for students through lessons and rehearsal plans, but they also serve as the architects of entire music programs. Like an architect, the teacher strives to build a strong foundation of knowledge. Like an architect, the teacher begins with a general plan in mind and oversees the construction of such a plan, sometimes making modifications along the way. Of course, the actual nature of this work varies depending upon the setting, and may involve a team instead of one person, relying on close collaboration with other music teachers or a music supervisor within a school district. In the beginning stages of a career, music teachers strive to gain confidence and comfort with daily and weekly planning. With experience, perspectives broaden (to return to the architectural metaphor, you see not just the features of a particular room but the shape of the entire building). Teachers develop and refine their expectations for the overall coherence and impact of the musical offerings supported by the school. When this important shift occurs, teachers often examine their music programs to evaluate whether the curriculum is *comprehensive, balanced, sequential,* and *relevant.* The first three of these adjectives have been cited most frequently and historically within the profession (Barrett, 2009; Mark & Gary, 2007); the concern for relevance reflects more recent dialogue (Kratus, 2007; Williams, 2007).

A *comprehensive* music curriculum is broad enough in scope to provide students with an equally broad range of ways to encounter and experience music. Through the curriculum, many types of *musical engagements* are made possible, including:

- Performing music through singing and playing instruments, as well as various settings for performance, including solo, small ensembles and chamber groups, and large ensembles we commonly know as bands, choirs, and orchestras;
- Listening to the music performed by others, including the development of skills and sensibilities to perceive musical qualities, think in sound, analyze music, and describe it with acuity and sophistication;

- Creating music through various forms of improvisation (from free improvisation to more structured or genre specific improvisation), arranging, composition;
- Representing music through the use of symbol systems (standard musical notation; graphic scores) or digital means;
- Studying the historical and cultural roots of music, the contributions of composers and cultures, the paths of influence and interrelatedness of musical ideas, forms, practices, and styles;
- Relating music to other forms of human expression and achievement, noting its commonalities with subjects "outside" of music as well as its distinctive qualities; and;
- Deepening our capacity to respond to music's expressive forms and feelings, and enhancing the meanings we derive from musical experience.[2]

A comprehensive music curriculum also reflects a teacher's (or overall music program's) wise sampling of musics to study that are drawn from the panoramic range of *musical styles, practices, and works* accessible to students. There are worlds of musics to explore, particularly when you start with a music teacher's personal and professional experience with music and expand that to embrace the realms of musical interests and experience that students bring with them to the music classroom. More than ever, due to the proliferation of musical ideas made accessible through live performance and mediated outlets, teachers can select increasingly diverse repertoires of works to perform and study. Imagine how these repertoires are expanded by the works that students create and choose themselves. Reimer's criteria of craftsmanship, sensitivity, imagination, and authenticity might be useful to guide this selection of music for classroom exploration.

A comprehensive music curriculum also addresses the **elements and forms of music.** Traditionally, these elements have included melody, rhythm, harmony, timbre, articulation, dynamics, texture and the ways that these elements are combined through varying musical forms and structures. Sound is the definitive core of the music curriculum, distinguishing music education from the rest of school subjects. Learning how properties of musical sound shape the patterns and complexities of music is integral to curricular work. Student understanding depends on how music moves and works.

If a comprehensive curriculum embraces a wide variety of musical engagements; musical styles, practices, and works; and musical elements and forms; then *balance* in the curriculum is a matter of emphasis. Balance is achieved when teachers align their curricular goals with the resources, opportunities, and constraints that influence curricular decisions, and make informed decisions about what to include and what to exclude. A balanced curriculum also involves weighing curricular decisions in light of the overarching philosophy of the school and community, teacher expertise, student interests, and practical considerations of space, funding, instructional time, and scheduling. No single school program can encompass the ever-expanding array of musical possibilities. A balanced program requires wisdom and care. A mixed sampler of offerings that is too eclectic can result in a music curriculum that merely introduces students to musical ideas through fleeting and superficial exposure. A program that is too narrowly focused at the other end can result in a restricted menu of opportunity and understanding. Questions related to balance focus on the proportion of elective and required courses, the range of opportunities offered, and the degree to which they are available for students at various levels of experience and interest.

A *sequential* music curriculum attends to the development of key understandings, skills, and habits in a systematic fashion to support students' musical development. The path for encountering musical ideas, from simple to complex, is chosen based on teachers' deliberations concerning:

- Students' development, and knowledge about their capabilities from early childhood through adolescence;
- Musical considerations, as teachers make decisions based on the challenges and sophistication of the music to be studied;
- Sensitivity to determine *when* learners best encounter certain musical ideas; and
- Personal knowledge, experience, and preferences of teachers, who organize the content in ways that make sense.

A classic notion of curricular ordering has been that of the spiral curriculum, in which students form increasingly differentiated and sophisticated understandings of music by encountering key ideas repeatedly but at more challenging levels (See Thomas, 1971).

Finally, *relevance* is a relatively new adjective to be cited in speaking about the music curriculum. The inclusion of relevance reflects the profession's desire to bridge the gap between the musics students encounter in school with the musics they encounter outside of school. Such efforts seek to incorporate popular, or vernacular, musics in the curriculum, as well as a range of cultural traditions and musical practices that have not traditionally been included in school music programs. Another aspect of relevance has to do with the role of music in the lives of individuals. Children's early years are infused with musical experiences, even before they enter formal schooling. The influences of the home, extended family, community, media, and societal milieu constitute a platform of understanding; the young child builds on this platform when making sense of a music class.

Relevance also speaks to the way that music programs prepare students to continue their musical involvements once they are no longer enrolled in school music programs. To account for relevance, teachers must keep in mind the lasting impression of making and studying music, and how the student moves toward an independent and fulfilling musical life beyond the boundaries of the program itself. Relevance is a key principle in the contemporary movement within the profession to foster lifelong learning, community music, and adult engagement in music. The school curriculum can be the foundation for this long and satisfying presence of music in our lives.

TAKE ACTION 6.4
A Panel on Building Music Programs

This Take Action is suggested once you have completed a significant number of observations, have gained experience working with a number of teachers across various settings, or have completed field experiences or student teaching.

Organize a panel of experienced music teachers and music supervisors, if available. Identify participants who have participated on curriculum writing committees or task forces, if possible. When generating a list of invitees, consider individuals who teach at different levels (elementary, middle, high school), in different schools or districts, and in different areas (general music, band, choir, orchestra, other areas). Seek out multiple points of view.

Using the discussion on the comprehensive, balanced, sequential, and relevant curriculum as a guide, prepare a roster of questions that you can send to the participants in advance to guide their preparation. You may also wish to ask the participants to send or bring copies of curriculum documents they have had a hand in creating, or other curricular frameworks they have used (or perhaps discarded) as their priorities have shifted over time. Organize, publicize, and carry out the event. The notes you take during the panel presentation will be informative as you develop a clearer picture of program development, or curriculum writ large.

After the panel, summarize your insights about serving as an architect of the music curriculum. In what ways did the panel participants enhance your understanding of the comprehensive, balanced, sequential, and relevant curriculum? How will you draw upon these insights as you prepare for this eventual responsibility of building a music program?

Studying the Commonplace of the Learner

The role of a learner is a role you currently hold, and one that you will continue to experience as a teacher committed to lifelong learning. It is a role with which you are intimately familiar. But because of this level of comfort and familiarity in the role of a learner, care must be given to avoid assumptions about learning based only on our own personal experiences. For example, as a student, you may find the teaching styles of certain professors to be particularly effective, and you recognize that in these contexts you develop deep understandings about the subject. Yet not every student in that course may find that professor's approach to be effective. As Delpit describes in the quote at the beginning of the chapter, every student enters a learning experience from a very personal and individual viewpoint.

If, then, learning (like teaching) is indeed a highly personalized phenomenon, what can we know and understand about learners? What principles and ideas can we accept as generalizable? Historically, learners and learning processes have been studied by looking through the lenses of various theoretical perspectives. You are, or will become, familiar with the ideas of many of these theories, models, and taxonomies of learning, such as Piaget's developmental theory, Vygotsky's theory of learning as a sociocultural phenomenon, Bandura's theory of social learning, Bruner's model of discovery learning, Gagné's categories of learning, and Bloom's cognitive taxonomy, to name a few. Recent work in early childhood has focused on Developmentally Appropriate Practice (DAP) principles. In the field of music, Edwin Gordon developed, and has continued to refine, a theory specifically related to music learning. Alongside these theorists are those who approach the learner and learning process through the idea of modalities of learning—aural, visual, and kinesthetic.

An awareness of the importance not only of knowing *how* students learn, but also of recognizing that students' characteristics influence the ways they engage in educational experiences provides another vantage point for learning about learners. Understandings of student diversity and student exceptionalities provide essential insights for developing a student-centered curriculum. This is the basis for "differentiated instruction," culturally responsive pedagogy, and "readiness" for learning, among many others. These understandings challenge and enable teachers to find ways to draw all students into the life of the classroom and to create a culture that acknowledges and addresses the needs of all students.

These theories and perspectives expand our knowledge about students and ways they learn. A personal orientation to understanding learners and learning processes moves us beyond knowing *about*, and positions the learner as the central informant and the primary source of information and insights. Understanding learners now becomes a process of knowing *in* and *within*—through the student's eyes. What does the student believe he or she needs to know? To experience? To understand? What happens to the curriculum with the student at the center? How do students see school music relating to the music in their lives outside of school? What does the music class feel like from his or her perspective? What meaning do students assign to school music experiences? What kinds of experiences do students find generative? Vibrant? What is the residue of the experiences students have with school music? We can begin to answer these questions by going directly to the students and attempting to uncover their perceptions and beliefs regarding their educational experiences and the ways those school experiences connect to their lived experiences outside of school.

The diagram shown in Figure 6.4 (Barrett, 2005) represents a reconceptualized view of curriculum planning that places students' understanding in the center of teachers' thinking about the relationships of school music programs to students' lived experiences outside of school, as well as their lifelong engagement in music. It was developed to contrast with more prevalent models of curriculum planning that typically start with preparatory steps for teachers to address before the curriculum is "delivered" to students, including diagnosing needs, formulating objectives, selecting and organizing content, and determining strategies for evaluating learning (Taba, 1962). Although logical steps are useful, they may miss the mark entirely

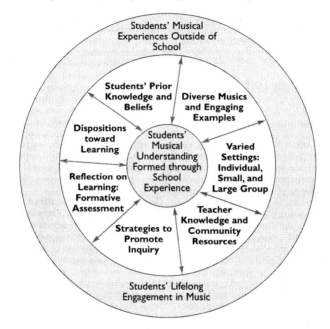

FIGURE 6.4. A Reconceptualized View of Curriculum.
Figure from p. 23 of article by J. R. Barrett, "Planning for Understanding: A Reconceptualized View of the Music Curriculum," *Music Educators Journal*, March 2005. Copyrighted © 2005 by Music Educators National Conference. Reprinted with permission.

if they assume students to be blank slates and recipients of the curriculum. In the diagram, the sections between the center and the outside circle are components of the curriculum to be considered in fostering this meaningful interaction.

Listening to the voices of students to understand their educational experiences is a fairly recent phenomenon in educational research. Cliff Schimmels gives us an example of his attempt to understand and to identify better with the lives of high school students (1985). Dr. Schimmels, at the time a 44-year-old university education professor, took a sabbatical from his university position and enrolled in a public school as a ninth grader, where he attended classes, ate in the cafeteria, and basically lived the life of a ninth grader every day for several weeks. His description of his experiences captures insights into the ways that students interpret and relate to curriculum, teachers, other students, and the institutional expectations that each of these aspects contribute to the learning experience.

The musical lives of young children became the focus for Patricia Shehan Campbell's (1998) narrative of her ethnographic work on the playground of Vista Elementary School. She describes her goal as follows:

> Through a combination of what I'd hoped would be nonreactive, unobtrusive observations and interviews with children in rather free-flowing

conversations, I decided that I would direct my efforts toward knowing children, their music, and the meaning of their musical behaviors, thoughts, and interests. It was a rational decision to cut to the quick, to consult with children as the primary sources of what I needed to know. I would go from and return to my own perspective as teacher and parent, and figure ways of fitting what insights children might offer on their musical lives into thoughts about their education and schooling. The mission set and the course laid out, the mysteries of musical children began to unravel themselves to me. (1998, p. 4)

Throughout her narrative Campbell presents the expressed thoughts and musical behaviors of children—both what they have learned and what they have spontaneously created. She discovered what level of value these children assign to music, and ways that music is socially and culturally meaningful to children.

In a similar manner, you can gain a greater sense of a student's perspective by carrying out a shadow study as part of your observation time. A shadow study is an inquiry strategy designed to obtain in-depth information about an individual or a group of individuals. Typically shadow studies in education occur when an observer (researcher, teacher, student teacher or education student) follows, or shadows, a teacher or a student through an entire day or series of days. The rich insights you will gain through a shadow study will expand your understanding of Schwab's commonplaces, and particularly of the learner.

One of the primary goals in conducting a shadow study is to get as close as possible to the individual or group being studied, without interfering with the work of that individual or group. Shadow studies attempt to gain the view from below (Katz, 1992), that is, the perspective of the individuals directly involved in, and affected by, the program, the school context, the curriculum, interactions with the teacher, or any other aspect of the educational experience.

TAKE ACTION 6.5
Connecting with Students' Perspectives: A Shadow Study

The purpose of this Take Action is to investigate a particular student's lived experience in school by arranging to do a shadow study. This study can take place with a student at any level of K-12 education. The broad purpose of this shadow study is to attempt to see educational experiences from the student's perspective.

Preliminary Steps for a Shadow Study

- Arrange to observe in a music class for a series of observations over time.
- Your initial observations will be general observations similar to those you have previously conducted. Take note of the context. Describe general characteristics of the students as a group. What general impressions

do you have of the context and the ways the students interact within that context? How do students relate to the curriculum? The subject matter?

- Following the preliminary observations (2–3), select a specific student as your focus for the next three to four observations. While you continue to observe the classroom in a holistic way, frequently take note of this specific student.

Conducting the Shadow Study

- Record what you see. Stevenson (1998) indicated it is not necessary to have prior experience in conducting a shadow study, but focus and attentiveness to detail is very important. As you observe a particular student, you may want to record field notes every 5–7 minutes, describing what you notice about the student at that point, the context, and your impressions in the moment.
- Take note of:
  - Interactions between the student and other students, music teachers, administrators, staff, volunteers, etc. How does the student engage with the music (subject matter)? How does context of the music classroom seem to affect the student's participation in the activities of the music class?
  - The level of engagement of the student. What conditions or interactions seem particularly to engage the student and create a sense of vibrancy? At any time is there a noticeable *lack* of vibrancy? Can you identify factors contributing to the level of engagement?
  - Curious, unusual or surprising events. What do you see that you did not expect to see?

"Unpacking" the Shadow Study

- Write a report of your study, including descriptive and interpretive aspects. Descriptive information should include contextual factors as well as a report of what you saw throughout your focus on this student's experiences. Interpretive aspects should relate what you can infer based on what you observed. Consider questions such as: Where, when, and under what conditions did the "signs of life" or educational vibrancy occur? What surprised you? What curious or unusual events did you observe? What did you see that you did not expect? Conclude your report with an overall summary of your reflections on the experience. What insights do you believe you gained through this study?
- After writing your report, locate and read the research studies that are briefly described in this section of Chapter 6 (Focus on Research 6.2 and 6.3). How does reading these studies influence your own observations and interpretations from your shadow study?

- Consider the previous discussion of curriculum in this chapter and reflect on this final question regarding your shadow study: To what extent did the curriculum (the planned activities, tasks, etc.) allow educationally vibrant experiences to occur?

To extend the work you have begun in uncovering students' perspectives, you may wish to conduct a follow-up interview with the student at the center of your shadow study to gain a deeper understanding of this individual, or you may wish to interview a different student for a more wide-ranging view. In either situation, a student interview holds great potential for you to develop a deeper understanding of students' perceptions about school, learning, and the role of music in their educational experience.

TAKE ACTION 6.6
Connecting with Students' Perspectives: Interview

The purpose of this Take Action is for you to gain greater understanding of students' musical and scholastic lives by conducting a student interview.

Preparing for the Interview

- Return to Table 2.1—*Ideas for Generating Interview Questions* and Take Action 2.1: *Gaining Insight from Interviewing Teachers in the Field.* Consider what you have learned about interviewing based on the interviews you may have already conducted.
- With the assistance of teachers and/or parents, identify and contact a student to interview. (Review Appendix 1: Ethics of Going Into The Field.) If possible, obtain permission to do an audio recording of the interview.
- Arrange a location for the interview. Use a location that is comfortable and known to the student, such as a classroom or the school media center. If it is not possible to do the interview in person, set a time for a phone call.
- Create a list of open-ended interview questions. Review Table 2.1 for categories you may wish to use as organizers for your questions. Questions should be worded in an age-appropriate manner. Sample questions for this interview can be found in Table 6.1.

A semi-structured approach to developing your interview may be most beneficial for your purposes. A semi-structured interview consists of questions in broad categories, such as the samples presented in Table 6.1. These

TABLE 6.1 Sample Questions for Interviewing a Student

Categories	Examples
Behaviors	*What do you enjoy doing when you are not in school? What kind of music do you listen to? What is (are) your favorite movies? TV shows? Foods? Sports? Video games? Books?*
Opinions/Values	*What are the most important things you are learning in school this year? What interests you most? What are your favorite subjects? If you could change anything about school what would it be? If you could choose any occupation what would it be? Do you enjoy listening to music?*
Feelings	*What aspect of school is most exciting or enjoyable to you? Least enjoyable? How does listening to different kinds of music make you feel?*
Knowledge	*What kinds of experiences in your classes best help you learn? What are the things you do when you study on your own? Do you play any musical instrument(s)? How do you practice? What works best to help you learn new pieces of music?*
Sensory	*When you watch a music video, what do you remember most—what you see or what you hear? When you play or sing music, do you pay more attention to watching the notes or listening to yourself?*
Background Demographics	*How many brothers and sisters do you have? Have you always lived in this city? What school(s) have you attended? Are members of your family musical? Have you traveled very much?*

questions form the basis of the interview, but there is flexibility in that, as the interviewer, you may or may not ask all of the questions based on how the student responds. It may be that the student's response will lead you to ask questions not on your list, but the list of questions serves as a guide to allow you to return to your focus when appropriate. As stated in Take Action 2.1, it is important to be flexible enough to "go with the flow" and yet recognize when to return to your prepared questions.

Conducting the Interview

■   Maintain a conversational, inviting tone with the student.

- Prepare your list of questions, leaving space to jot down notes about the student's responses.
- Record the interview if you have obtained prior permission to do so.
- Focus on the student; be intentionally inviting in your non-verbal communication (body language, facial expressions).
- Pay close attention to the student's words, but also tone of voice and body language. Be observant as well as a good listener.
- Students may range from very verbose to giving very brief answers. Be prepared to ask the "why" questions to encourage students to further explore the ideas.

Sharing What You Have Discovered

- Review your interview notes and recording immediately, clarifying and filling in any gaps in your notes.
- Write a report of your interview. Begin with a brief section summarizing the demographic information you learned and observed about this student. Follow this with a summary of the questions and student's responses.
- Depending on the age of the student you interviewed, you may want to send the student a copy of the interview report. Ask the student to confirm or to make corrections to insure that the report accurately reflects the student's responses.
- Prepare to share your report. In class, work with a classmate or small group and discuss your reports. What do you find similar? Different? What can you infer about students as learners from your interviews?
- Based on your small group work, report to the entire class. As a class, create a representation in the style of a concept map as a means of creating a collective impression of similarities and differences in students' behaviors, beliefs, values, knowledge, and backgrounds. What can you infer from this? Can you make any generalizations from this? How does this reinforce the need for, and value of, seeking the students' perspectives?

As a lifelong learner and a future music educator, an essential aspect of your work will be purposefully continuing to learn about students—who they are, how they learn, the ways they interact with Schwab's commonplaces, and the value they give music in their lives. Focus on Research 6.2 and 6.3 demonstrate ways that researchers have explored different aspects of students' musical lives in school.

FOCUS ON RESEARCH 6.2
Diva Irina: An English Language Learner in High School Choir

Regina Carlow (2006) conducted a collective case study exploring the perceptions of five English-language learner (ELL) high school students. For this particular study, Carlow focused primarily on the experiences of Irina Choi, a recent immigrant from Kazakhstan and a choral student. The choral class was a non-auditioned choir, and the monolingual chorus teacher had taught at this school for four years.

The year-long ethnographic case study arose from Carlow's perception of a tension between the traditions of school choral programs and the choral experiences of immigrant learners. Her overarching research question was "What are the musical experiences of immigrant students who sing in high school choir?" Three specific questions further defined the study:

1. What are the previous and present musical experiences of immigrant students who sing in high school choir?
2. How do immigrant students perceive the repertoire, rehearsals, performance requirements, and practices of high school choir?
3. To what extent and in what ways do immigrant students feel they belong to, contribute to, and benefit from the high school choir?

Carlow stated, "To capture the perspectives of these students accurately, I initiated and maintained a dialogue and interplay of written and spoken reflections with the participants over a 10-month period" (2006, p. 66). Her data collection included interviews with the five participants as well as with other nonimmigrant students, teachers, and administrators, student and teacher surveys, video-analysis, and field notes from over 20 hours of observations of the traditions and customs in the choral classroom and rehearsals. Carlow transcribed all interviews and field notes, and in analyzing and coding the data created files for each student as well as files for concerts, rehearsals, and general site data.

Using a narrative approach, Carlow introduces Irina to the reader through two scenarios: one reflecting a confident student singing a Russian pop song for International Night at the school, and the second describing a bored, detached young girl slouched in a chair in choir class. These two sides to Irina are detailed in "Hearing Irina's Voice," where Carlow presents the reader with the frustrations expressed by Irina.

Although Irina had happily participated in choir prior to coming to the United States, Irina attributed her current dissatisfaction to boring music, the teaching style, and being "forced" to attend concerts. She felt that she should be in a more advanced choir, believing that the teacher held little regard for this non-auditioned choir. Carlow found that underlying Irina's discontent was a perception of a lack of caring and meaningful interaction with the teacher. While Irina stated that she "liked singing," as exemplified by her participation in the International Night show, she did not like choir. Her perception of herself as a "pop" singer shaped her musical identity.

In summarizing this study, Carlow points out the need for music educators to be aware of the wide-ranging beliefs and experiences ELL students bring to the classroom. She emphasizes the importance of taking into account cultural and individual differences, and "validating and affirming all students' previous musical and educational backgrounds" (Carlow, 2006, p. 75), while seeking to form meaningful relationships.

FOCUS ON RESEARCH 6.3
An Exploratory Investigation of Three Middle School General Music Students' Beliefs About Music Education (Wayman), and *The Meaning of Music Education to Middle School General Music Students* ([Wayman] Davis)

In 2004, using the theories of Multiple Intelligence and of Reasoned Action, Wayman interviewed three middle school general music students in an attempt to determine how these students view music education. The three students were selected from a required, non-performance based music class, a population underrepresented in music education research.

The general music class provided opportunities for students to read and compose music, play classroom instruments, including drums and guitars, and learn about music history. From this class, 10 students were initially recommended for the study. Wayman asked these students to complete a questionnaire that allowed her to select students who did not already have backgrounds in music outside of school. Over a two-month period, Wayman interviewed the three students selected, and also observed the music class. The interviews, using open-ended questions, were recorded and transcribed for coding and identifying themes and categories.

All three students believed that they, as well as their parents, considered music "fun" and less serious than core classes—the work is considered easier. Students also expressed the shared belief that they were less talented than other students, and music class is more important for the talented students. Likewise they all identified entertainment as the purpose for music, stating that without music it would be "boring."

Wayman concludes her report of this study by pointing out the implications of these themes for teachers. While music educators hope students find joy in music, the perception that music is not a serious subject is problematic. The issue of talent can also be challenging as students, even though stating they enjoy music, demonstrate low self-efficacy in music through statements such as "I can't sing." Viewing music's role as entertainment raises questions about music education reaching the goal of aesthetic education. In each of these dilemmas raised by the students' responses, teachers must look for ways to reinforce positive beliefs about music education, while raising students' perceptions of self-efficacy in music.

In 2009, Wayman (now Davis) revisited her questions about the meanings students find in music. Again focusing on middle school general music students, her research questions asked, "What meaning do middle school general music students derive from their musical education, and do underlying dimensions exist in its meaning? If these dimensions do exist, what are they?" This study, a large-scale survey with 762 students from eight different states, used the Music Meaning Survey developed by Davis. This survey contained 50 statements of meaning to which students responded using a four-point scale ranging from "really disagree" to "really agree."

Following factor analysis of the data, Davis identified four categories of meaning students find in their school music experiences. Vocational emerged as the strongest factor and reflected students' interests in being performers and actively engaged in music. Academic, the second highest factor, related to students' interests in learning to read music, and to learn about composers and genres of music. Belongingness and agency, the third and fourth factors, reinforce understandings about middle school students' desires to affiliate with peers, and to develop a sense of self-confidence in what they do. The students in this study felt being in music class increased their sense of belongingness and agency.

Davis concluded by emphasizing that middle school general music students do find general music to be a meaningful experience, and that music education can provide multiple and varied benefits in the lives of the students. These positive perspectives can carry over into greater involvement in music outside of school. Additionally, based on the meaning students find in general music, Davis advocated for the inclusion and expansion of general music courses in the middle school curriculum.

These studies illustrate three of the many ways you can gain insight into students' perspectives on their lives and lived experiences in music classes. As these students interact with teachers, other students, and the curriculum and subject matter, the power and impact of the context in which these interactions occur quickly becomes apparent.

Studying the Commonplace of Context

Q

AT CLOSE RANGE 6.1
A Tale of Two Schools

As an elementary general music teacher, I teach at two schools every day—one in the morning (Daybreak Elementary) and one in the afternoon (Sunset Elementary). I see firsthand how each school functions as a distinct community from my vantage point as an itinerant teacher. At Daybreak, teachers usually drop off and pick up their children to music at the appointed time and use the music time to work in their own rooms, often with the doors closed. I rarely see teachers working together on joint projects. Even the staff meetings seem especially business-like and individualistic as we march through the agenda. At Sunset, there is always some new idea germinating in the halls or in the teachers' lounge. Teachers spend time conversing with one another, lingering in doorways, sharing teaching materials and techniques, and discussing student concerns across classrooms. The entire school works on behalf of joint projects such as special events and performances. These differences in my two school environments influence my music program. At Daybreak, my music classroom stands alone and so do I. At Sunset, I am frequently asked for my opinions and ideas as I collaborate with others on behalf of the students. In turn, my colleagues support my musical goals for the children because they are aware of what I hope to accomplish. Even when I plan thoughtful lessons for a particular grade level to teach at both schools, the students' musical experience seems very different because the schools are so different.

Schools as Cultures

When we think of schools, we usually conjure up mental images of the schools we have attended, and these images constitute our typical, or normative, idea of what schools are like. Common sense suggests that schools differ in location, physical appearance and layout, design, age, size, and community demographics. These factors influence educational programs such as the music curriculum. Studying these tangible characteristics is revealing and informative. Another approach to understanding contextual differences relies on viewing particular schools through anthropological, biological, and sociological lenses. Each school functions as a distinctive, dynamic, and discernible culture, much as the elementary general music teacher noted in the preceding paragraph. The noted art educator Elliot Eisner has written eloquently about this notion, pointing to the role of the arts in shaping this context for learning:

> The term *culture* is said to have hundreds of meanings. Two are particularly relevant to education, one anthropological, the other biological. A culture in the

anthropological sense is a shared way of life. But the term *culture* in a biological sense refers to a medium for growing things. Schools, I believe, like the larger society of which they are a part, function as cultures in both senses of the term. They make possible a shared way of life, a sense of belonging and community, and they are a medium for growing things, in this case children's minds. How schools are organized, what is taught in them, the kinds of norms they embrace, and the relationships they foster among adults and children all matter, for they all shape the experiences that students are likely to have and in the process influence who children will become. Experience is central to growth because experience is the medium of education. Education, in turn, is the process of learning to create ourselves, and it is what the arts, both as a process and as the fruits of that process, promote. Work in the arts is not only a way of creating performances and products; it is a way of creating our lives by expanding our consciousness, shaping our dispositions, satisfying our quest for meaning, establishing contact with others, and sharing a culture. (Eisner, 2002, p. 3)

Obviously, the culture of a school is created by the participants in the school as well as influential members of the school community in which the school is located. The traditions, symbols, expectations, rituals, norms and values of a school contribute to a shared identity and are communicated through the events, actions, policies, and practices within the school. Taken together, the culture of the school can be examined through "the customs, practices, and traditions that characterize, distinguish, and give stability to a group" (Bullough & Gitlin, 2001, p. 112). Music teachers often encounter and uncover the implicit cultural assumptions of a school community by investigating how music is valued in the curriculum. Consider, for example, a middle school music teacher who advocates the study of popular music, who accepts a position in a school community where popular music is not seen as legitimate, or a choral educator who tries to organize madrigal and chamber ensembles in a community where large-scale musical theater productions are the norm. What of an elementary general music teacher who uses movement in a school where students' religious practices prohibit their participation, or an instrumental music educator who stresses concert band when the community views the marching band as the main justification for the program? Barresi and Albrecht (2000) recommend that music teachers study school culture, since this is a way in which teachers can influence the way the community values and supports musical experiences for its students. They suggest:

Any music teacher wishing to affect or change the community culture must first determine and assess the kinds of community organizational structures in operation; the shared values, beliefs, and norms of the members of these structures; and the degree to which the teacher's personal goals and philosophy for the music program match or accommodate those of the community and the school. (Barresi & Albrecht, 2000, p. 129)

FOCUS ON RESEARCH 6.4
Looking at Schools as Musical Cultures

Chee-Hoo Lum and Patricia Shehan Campbell conducted an ethnographic study of an elementary school to investigate the notion that school cultures are infused by the musical expressions of children and adults, which constitute the "sonic surrounds" of the school. The purpose of their study was to "gain an understanding of the nature and context of rhythmic and melodic expressions made by children, and heard by children, too, as emanating from other children as well as adults within the school environment" (Lum & Campbell, 2007, p. 33).

The researchers selected an urban elementary school in a large city on the West coast as the site for the study. Over a six-month period, Lum and Campbell observed, recorded, and generated field notes to capture first-through third-grade children's musical behaviors and utterances on the playground, in the hallways, and in classrooms. Their ethnographic study is based on what they learned from a combined total of 72 hours of observation and transcriptions of spontaneous musical moments, songs, rhythms, games, and movement activity. Guided by the notion of soundscapes, or the array of sounds that "envelop people in their daily lives at home and in their various work and recreational contexts" (2007, p. 32), the researchers examined their field notes to develop analytic categories that framed the research report.

In the study, Lum and Campbell provide detailed descriptions of five main themes:

- children's rhythmic play,
- melodic musical utterances,
- creations and re-creations of familiar songs,
- the use of music as a social signal, and
- the use of music to facilitate learning.

Their data substantiate how music contributes to socialization as children play and interact with one another throughout the school day as well as the way that teachers weave musical moments into lessons to enliven learning activities.

Lum and Campbell provide vivid evidence that music is an integral part of children's daily experience, and that students help to create the sonic environment as well as participate in formal instruction offered by the school. Teachers who attend to children's musical culture can more readily build on what children bring with them to the classroom. Building rich knowledge of the multiple dimensions of a school community involves knowing "both what it visually appears to be and what it sounds like. Thus, knowing the school and the children within the school may in no small measure be based on careful examination of its sonic fabric, this soundscape that is the result of the musical behaviors of children and teachers" (p. 32).

Becoming savvy about school culture and the way it influences music teaching and learning takes experience and discernment, but such study can yield valuable insights for teachers who want to effect change or preserve valuable traditions in their music programs.

Shifting our Perspectives on School Contexts

Think of a zoom lens on a camera for a moment and how you can shift your perspective on a scene by alternately zooming in and zooming out. The educational philosopher Maxine Greene writes about how shifting our perspective on schools changes our relationship to schools and those who inhabit them. She draws from literature, in particular a novel by Thomas Mann, to explore the concept of seeing the world "small" or seeing it "big" (Greene, 1995). To see things small is to view schools at a distance, stepping back in order to bring the entire landscape into view. This is the perspective of policy-makers, who must make decisions about schools' interests collectively as if they were surveying them from the window of an airplane. When operating from the most benevolent and well-informed stance, educational policies support progressive social change. They reflect Dewey's pedagogic creed that everyone interested in education "insist upon the school as the primary and most effective interest of social progress and reform" (Archambault, 1964, p. 438). Adopting a systems view of schools helps us to see how any particular school is a reflection of societal values and mores as well as the traditions and innovations that are currently held as important in any professional field or subject matter area.

To see schools up close, or to see them "big" as Maxine Greene would say, means that we also need to zoom in on the particularities of any given school and the students and teachers who inhabit it, "in close contact with details" (Greene, 1995, p. 10). Developing understanding of the particular complexities of school life is as crucial for teachers new to the field as it is for seasoned professionals. In building this knowledge, teachers become more responsive to students' lived experiences, and also more cognizant of the ways that ideas "from outside" influence daily interactions, priorities, and motivations for growth. Greene speaks to the necessity for teachers "to learn how to move back and forth, to comprehend the domains of policy and long-term planning while also attending to particular children, situation-specific understandings, the unmeasurable, and the unique" (p. 11).

Consider the following diagram, then, as a representation of four vantage points for the study of schools. Although these four are shown with boundaries for each ring of the diagram, influential ideas travel back and forth as if the lines were actually permeable membranes. Schools are influenced by society as they in turn influence students' capacities to act upon society. Teachers mediate these ideas through the curriculum and make them meaningful through experience.

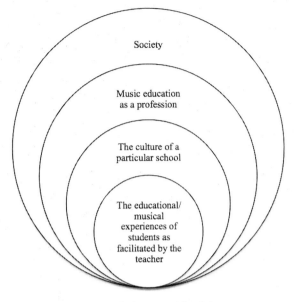

FIGURE 6.5. Embedded Circles—School and Society

TAKE ACTION 6.7
Developing a School Profile

Engage in school study. Choose a school that you can visit repeatedly, or use this opportunity to get to know a field study or practicum site with greater nuance and complexity. The purpose of this exercise is to develop a profile of a selected school that illuminates how the contextual "surrounds" of the school shape what is learned and taught. Choose one or more of the following strategies as starting places for your investigation:

- Examine the stated mission of the school, stated online or on paper. What educational values are communicated in print?
- Consult databases to profile the demographic characteristics of a school,[3] such as setting—urban, rural, suburban; number of students; number of teachers.
- Profile the teachers (or music faculty) by socioeconomic status, ethnicity, race, gender, years of experience in teaching, years of experience at this school.
- Observe the teachers in classroom interactions with students. Use the Embedded Squares diagram to focus your attention on teacher(s), students, subject matter, and milieu (See Take Action 6.1). Keep in mind Miranda, Robbins and Stauffer's ethnographic and portraiture methods.

- Observe teachers in other settings besides the classroom. What kinds of interactions and conversations characterize teachers' meetings, talk in the teachers' lounge, informal encounters?
- Examine the hallways, public spaces, and bulletin boards for clues of shared culture and school values, such as awards and tributes, recognitions, accomplishments of students, faculty, staff.
- What reflections of policies, initiatives, and social trends from "outside" the school do you see reflected within the school?
- Gather information about the rituals and traditions of the school.
- Look for signs of the musical and artistic culture of the school outside of the music room itself.
- Listen for the sounds made within the school by students, teachers, and various forms of media. Keep Lum and Campbell's soundscapes in mind.
- Profile administrators' or parents' involvement in the musical culture of the school.

As you engage in school study, differences in school culture will become apparent through comparative analysis of more than one setting. Much like the elementary general music teacher in the opening vignette of this section, strive to become an astute observer and interpreter of school culture. Take an anthropologist's stance to investigate how schools "work" and how teaching and learning is influenced by shared values and beliefs. As Eisner implies, you can then begin to influence that culture as you contribute to the social interactions that provide the medium for growing minds and persons. Similar to the ethnographic approaches used by Lum and Campbell or Miranda, Robbins and Stauffer, many of these interactions and connections will become apparent through regular, sustained observation and contact with teachers and students in the same school or district.

AT CLOSE RANGE 6.2
The Philosophy of an Intermediate School as an Invitation for School Study

Many schools or school districts develop philosophies or mission statements that convey the values and intentions of the school to persons inside and outside the school. They are usually developed by consensus, and at best, distill the values that teachers, administrators, and the broader community hold for students in succinct and sometimes inspiring forms. Read this overview of the philosophy of the Northshore School, a school serving fifth and sixth grade students located in a suburban setting near a large metropolitan area.

Philosophy of the Northshore School[1]

We believe that:

- *The primary focus of education should be on intellectual growth with attention to the emotional, social, physical, and cultural development of students.*
- *Educating the early adolescent requires thoughtful and deliberate decisions by the professional staff and the active collaboration of the learner, the family, and the larger community.*
- *Through guidance and example, every student should be encouraged to reach his or her maximum intellectual potential.*
- *Learning requires consistent effort, collaboration, and a genuine commitment.*
- *It is essential to create a learning environment where students are encouraged to engage in reflective, independent, analytical, and creative thinking.*
- *Students and adults need to understand the effect that each person can have on one another, on the community, and on the world.*
- *It is important to develop self-confidence, lasting relationships, and positive interpersonal skills.*
- *Our school community must foster an atmosphere of trust and a feeling that it is acceptable for students and staff to take risks, resulting in successes as well as failures in the process of learning.*
- *Children learn best when a teacher utilizes appropriate teaching styles, plans purposeful and sequential activities, communicates clear expectations, integrates learning, and relates the content to a child's interests and existing knowledge.*
- *It is important to practice the principles of a democratic community, to foster sound decision making, and to encourage students to make responsible contributions to the school, their environment, and the larger community.*
- *We must respect the diversity and recognize the commonality among people.*

The philosophy of the Northshore School, and the way that these beliefs were put into practice on a daily basis, was the subject of a school study for preservice teachers enrolled in a middle school general music course. Over a seven-week period, the preservice teachers observed and assisted small groups of fifth-grade students who were composing music for a large-scale interdisciplinary project at the school called the Extravaganza. *The music teacher in collaboration with the drama and dance teachers at the school created this project. Together, they invited community musicians from an Indonesian performance group to work with the fifth graders, who learned to play the gamelan as part of the project. Fifth graders in dance and drama groups brought Indonesian folk tales to life; the fifth grade composers were charged to compose original music on the gamelan to accompany the dance and dramatic action. At the heart of the project as conceived by the teachers was the notion that students take ownership of their learning, solving creative problems. The preservice teachers were asked to reconcile the stated philosophy of the school with their observations and insights having participated in the* Extravaganza *as well. As you read the excerpts that follow, keep the principles of the school's mission in mind.*

Jeff, who in addition to seeking his license to teach is an accomplished composer himself, concentrated on the way that the music teacher and her colleagues constructed a learning environment in which the fifth grade students could explore creative problem-solving. He spoke of the Extravaganza *as:*

> *a carefully wrought framework constructed by the teachers in advance and informed by experiences in previous years. This framework is always focused on having the students collaborate and solve problems* in order to make the project a success . . . *The teachers, instead of carefully designing all the tracks of learning, instructional strategies, and sequences of problem solving, only created a structure on their own; however, this was a structure that com-*pelled *the students to fill in the holes. The lines of the painting were drawn, but the colors were not even suggested. Additionally, the problems allowed to surface were not only real-world, but they were necessary to be solved. The students did not simply write music for situations because they were told to do so by the teacher, but because it was obvious to everyone that it was necessary. This is in part a result of teaching in a district with students who have been taught to be curious and who understand the results of working hard. The teachers at Northshore were able to turn over ownership of the project to students to such a degree that the problems* and *solutions belonged to them and functioned as a part of the larger creation.*

Jeff was also captivated by the ways that the project softened boundaries between school experience and life outside school walls, prompted especially through its focus on Indonesian music and the opportunity the students had to work with the guest artists.

> *Considering the project in light of authenticity brings up many different issues in music education. At first glance, it may seem impossible to ever make activities, units, or curriculums fully authentic. The teaching and learning will always take place within the confines of a school and will be found by the contextual characteristics found in Joseph Schwab's four commonplaces of the curriculum. However, in addition to its elusiveness, complete focus on authenticity, realism, and accuracy can lead to major philosophical and curricular dilemmas for the educator. Music education is not a laboratory; it is a space that is connected to the greater world and valid in its own right . . . I believe that objective is to cherish and enrich a dynamic learning space inside the school that is deeply connected with and co-dependent on the musical*

world that exists beyond its "confines." This does not mean that we simply learn about the "outside world." Instead, it requires that we engage musical cultures authentically, through real-world experiences that challenge us both as individuals and as members of communities. This was definitely a driving force behind this school project. I hope I can take these ideas and apply them to my teaching so I can create learning experiences that are as dynamic, holistic, and lasting as those we witnessed during this project.

In conducting a school study, Jeff tested the philosophic tenets of the school as he observed them in action, looking for ways that the principles animated the work of the arts teachers and middle school students involved in creating original music, choreography, and dramatic script and action to portray folk tales from Indonesian culture. Using the mission of the school as a framework invited reflection on the alignment of the teachers' beliefs with their practices. Jeff was able to see how the teachers created "a learning environment where students are encouraged to engage in reflective, independent, analytical, and creative thinking." In addition, he reflected on the school's integration of democratic principles with its commitment to real-life musical problems and experiences, and the reliance on culture bearers to bridge the gap between school and community. The school study provided the impetus for examining and expressing what preservice teachers saw, heard, felt, and experienced through their engagement with the project.

School Study from the Teachers' Point of View: Realms of Teachers' Work in Context

When we think of music teachers, we commonly think of someone standing in the front of a room filled with a large group of lively elementary or secondary students. This is the prominent image of teachers we have formed from our vantage points as students. In reality, the professional duties of a music teacher encompasses multiple overlapping contexts; we seldom get to peek "behind the scenes" to see the full extent and range of these duties. A useful model for representing a teacher's work in schools comes from Thiessen and Anderson (1999), who studied teachers in the midst of school reforms. They describe three realms of teachers' work that enhance our appreciation for the roles and responsibilities teachers assume. These realms are represented in Figure 6.6.

This diagram is particularly illuminating for thinking about music teachers in context, since music teachers are often called upon to build support for music programs and to collaborate with other teachers. Consider how work in the corridors involves many teachers, staff, and administrators represented among the school's roster of adults. Work across communities can also involve many other associations, institutions, community organizations, and agencies. These are further detailed in Take Action 6.8.

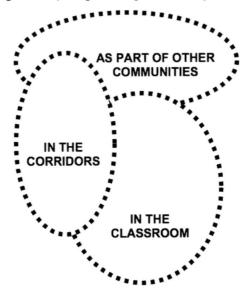

FIGURE 6.6. The Realms of Teachers' Work.
Adapted from Thiessen & Anderson, 1999.

TAKE ACTION 6.8
Realms Interview

You have built your understanding of teachers' lives and roles through various exercises throughout this book, including identifying characteristics of successful and unsuccessful teachers (Chapter 1); conducting interviews as a source of knowledge about teaching (Chapter 2); and interviewing beginning teachers (Chapter 3). As your understanding of music teaching has become more integrated and differentiated, this interview is focused on broadening understanding of the roles and responsibilities of teachers.

Develop a protocol that you will use to interview a music teacher about these overlapping realms of work. In addition to classroom responsibilities, develop questions to address:

■   The teacher's work "in the corridors" with teachers of other disciplines and subjects, other music teachers, school administrators, resource personnel, staff, and parents. This category can also lead to questions about collaborative projects, mentoring, and cross-disciplinary efforts.

■   The teacher's work "in other communities" including professional associations, community music organizations, collaboration with cultural institutions (symphony orchestra outreach programs, museums, libraries, media); school/university partnerships with nearby institutions of higher education; social agencies (perhaps in service learning projects); and government or state departments of education.

As portraits of music teachers' work across these realms emerge, consider asking questions such as the following:

- How do you allocate your professional energies across these realms of work, and what aspects of your work yield the most impact and influence?
- Over time, has the percentage of time and effort spent in these various realms shifted?
- How prepared did you feel to work across multiple arenas when you first began to teach?
- What are the challenges and satisfactions of working across realms?
- What are the benefits from taking on collaborative projects and/or new initiatives that take you and your students outside of the music room?

Read the interviews of other students in your class. Engage in dialogue about the expanded and multifaceted nature of music teachers' work. How does learning about initiatives in the corridor and in the community shift your attention as you prepare?

Becoming a Student of Music Teaching and Learning

In this last part of this book, we return to where we began: an examination of your self as a learner and as a student of music teaching and learning. To become a life-long learner in music education requires a disposition of ongoing analysis that involves studying the self and studying the different contexts that make up a teacher's personal/professional life (Schön 1983, 1987). Self and context study, we suggest, lies at the heart of constructing a personal orientation to music teaching and becoming a student of music education. One form of self-study often encountered throughout professional development in music education is the teaching portfolio.

Many music teacher preparation programs, regardless of theoretical orientation, require their students to construct a teaching portfolio that demonstrates what they have learned, what they know and what they can do. Campbell and Brummett (2002) note in their work with preservice music teachers that portfolios often take different forms depending upon purpose and goal. They identify three basic types: (a) the process-folio, (b) the product-folio, and (c) the process/product-folio. The overall purpose of the process-folio is to illustrate personal growth and change in thinking or to discuss a specific teaching/learning process supported with commentary and reflection. Product-folios are "summative," with the focus centered on "finished" products or culminating in representations of your learning, skills and abilities at a specific point in time. Process/product-folios, as the name suggests, are hybrids. Process/product-folios combine the elements of presenting what you know and can do in "finished" form and simultaneously demonstrating how thinking and skills have changed over time.

Samaras and Freese (2006) go further in suggesting other forms of self-study that highlight the interactional nature of self and context that teaching portfolios sometimes miss, especially teaching portfolios that take on standardized or institutionalized forms. Samaras and Freese include the following methodologies: (a) personal history study (similar to the Musical Circles in Take Action 1.2 found in Chapter 1); (b) visual and artistic-based representations of your background and beliefs and what you know and can do (concept maps, video-films, multi-media representations, performances, poems, for example); and (c) memory work (autobiographical inquiry accompanied by critical and reflective thinking). Similar to Campbell and Brummett's use of process/product-folios, Samaras and Freese suggest that teachers take opportunities to construct *developmental* portfolios—documented processes and artifacts that are stored, catalogued, described, and examined for teacher growth over a selected period of time.

Collectively each of the methodologies for studying self and context allows opportunities for teachers to reflect on their upbringings, as well as opportunities for teachers to acknowledge cultural and historical spaces that have contributed to shaping their own professional identities. Thus *personal* growth and development are important aims. In addition these methodologies highlight the importance of *professional* growth and development, particularly because they are situation specific. That is, a teacher's own classroom and working environments are the places from which reflection and action occur.

Furthermore, each of these methodologies serves as a stage for developing instructional techniques and for promoting classroom and school improvement. Especially helpful is focusing on the specific problems, concerns, and proficiencies that you are likely to encounter over the course of your career. When shared with colleagues and critical friends, traditions—including the "grammars of schooling" discussed in Chapter 5—that act as obstacles and hinder innovation can be identified and questioned. Plus, alternative ideas for curriculum and instructional design and development can be introduced. Each of these self and context study methodologies can be a starting point for both educational change and reform as well as for personal/professional renewal as discussed in Chapter 3.

Self and context study as an inquiring activity—including its *processes and products*—stands in contrast to teaching based on routine, method implementation, impulse, or tradition. It is a systematic and critical examination of a teacher's actions in a specific context designed to develop a more "consciously driven mode of a professional activity" (Samaras & Freese, 2006, p. 11). In Take Action 6.9 we invite you to begin to use a more systematic and sophisticated approach to clarifying your reasons for seeking a life in music teaching and for documenting your own growth by constructing a developmental portfolio.

TAKE ACTION 6.9
Developmental Portfolio

A developmental portfolio is a self and context study that focuses on questions or components of teaching that a teacher would like to improve. Often these teaching questions are related to professional or personal goals. Usually the study is bound by a specific time period. Depending upon what you want to improve, materials (for example, journals, video recordings, photographs of classroom, notes from conversations, student work, lessons, observations of peers, mentor feedback, interviews of students, notes from college classes, etc.) are collected and organized for analysis. In looking at the information and analyzing the materials, the goal is to focus on growth.

Getting Started

Gather and take a look at the interview reports, self-examinations, observation reports, research summaries, exercises and activities that you have either written or read as you worked your way through this book. (Appendix 2, *How to Use this Book* provides a detailed list of all the different investigative activities found in each chapter). As a collection of artifacts, these materials can be used to construct your own developmental portfolio.

Analyzing Materials

Study your collection. Evaluate your thinking and work. Think about the criteria you will use when making decisions about what "counts" as quality work or quality thinking. Ask yourself some "wonderings." For example, "I wonder what I have learned? I wonder how my thinking has changed about curriculum, about learners?" Or, ask more targeted questions. For example, "What areas of music teaching and learning do I still need to know about based upon what I know or understand right now?" Samaras and Freese (2006) offer some helpful questions when analyzing materials:

> What themes are common and are evident in your materials?
> Have earlier viewpoints, beliefs, or attitudes changed? What factors and
> experiences do you believe have contributed to the changes?
> What were your dilemmas?
> What metaphor best captures who you are as a teacher?
> What was your greatest "Ah-Ha?"
> What do you want to continue doing?
> What professional hopes, wishes remain unfulfilled?

Assembling Your Portfolio

- Prepare some type of representation of your growth. The easiest and most common method for assembling your portfolio is to put all of your materials into a three-ring notebook.
- A second option for assembling portfolio materials is to prepare items in a digital or electronic format. If you choose to create a digital portfolio, the options for display and design increase dramatically.
- Another option is to consider synthesizing your analysis using some of the forms suggested above for representing your work; artistic-based representations seem quite appropriate for students of music education.

Evidence of Impact

Developmental portfolios can be quite powerful when shared with others. The following are some ways to share your work and show evidence of impact.

- Share your portfolio with a partner or critical friends groups.
- Write a letter to a trusted friend or mentor about your professional journey. Then follow up with several conversations to discuss the process, and the changes that occurred.
- Give a presentation to a class, or to a significant individual in the profession such as a principal, cooperating teacher, student teacher mentor, faculty member, etc.

Big Question

In what ways does your portfolio show that you are on your way to becoming a music teacher with the necessary knowledge, skills and dispositions needed to address the needs of today's learners? In other words, how does your work identify, articulate and reflect the idea that a professional empowerment begins with curiosity about self and curiosity about context?

A central idea in this chapter has been the notion that teacher learning is significantly informed by practices and methodologies that explore self, learners and contexts. A major goal of the chapter has been to cultivate the disposition to engage in systematic and persistent investigation into your own teaching and professional environments in order to address problems of practice and avenues of change. Think about where you started in Chapter 1 and think about how your sophistication has increased in your understanding of the complexities of music teaching and learning as you worked your way through each chapter. Take a few moments to reflect on the following extract from *Little Gidding* by T.S. Eliot:

We shall not cease from exploration
And the end of all our exploring
Will be to arrive where we started
And know the place for the first time.
          T.S. Eliot—"Little Gidding"
    (the last of his *Four Quartets*), 1945

This often cited extract has much to say about trying to understand the world we inhabit. Perhaps the reason for its popularity is that the message is quite clear—the only way to know the world is to explore it. Similarly, it has been our contention that one of the most powerful ways to understand the musical and professional worlds we inhabit is to explore it. Unlike texts that survey different aspects of typical music programs (looking in on early childhood or band programs, for example) or detail step-by-step approaches to teaching music by focusing on technical competencies or identifying key attributes that "define" successful music programs, we have tried to ground your learning in the personal, the practical, and the interactive. As such, we have encouraged you to view music teaching and learning, as well as your current and future development as a music educator, as inquiry oriented, reflective, collaborative and constructive.

In closing, we invite you to "know your own landscape": to look at musical/educational experiences and their vitality through the eyes of students and others; to use your "zoom lenses" in order to gain flexibility in shifting perspectives; and to take actions toward self-empowerment and change agency in curriculum matters. Plus, we suggest that you explore and read on your own. Many, many topics remain to be examined and studied in learning and teaching music—classroom organization and management is an important topic; culturally responsive pedagogy and critical pedagogy are additionally important topics, as is teaching music through the lens of social justice. There are still others, and you can continue your professional development by looking into these topics, any or all of which could serve as starting points for curriculum inquiry. The *For Your Inquiry* at the end of the chapter lists some sources of interest.

Lastly, we encourage you to continue to question and reflect on matters related to yourself, to learners, to colleagues, to curriculum, and to communities. We encourage you to take a place in the profession as a lifelong learner and an agent of change who is empowered by a solid understanding of self while at the same time capable of imagining "visions of what can be possible" for the students you will serve.

For Your Inquiry

Boardman, E. (Ed.). (2002). *Dimensions of musical learning and teaching: A different kind of classroom.* **Reston, VA: MENC: The National Association for Music Education.**

Edited by long-time leader in music teacher education Eunice Boardman, this book contains 13 chapters, authored by prominent teacher educators representing diverse specializations—early childhood, general music, special education, technology, choral, band, and instrumental music education. Drawing upon contemporary social and constructivist theories in education, each chapter discusses the role *learning* plays in effective music teaching. A more substantive text on music teaching and learning that incorporates research, practical suggestions, illustrations and examples would be difficult to find. This is a "must" for the professional.

Campbell, P. S. (1998). *Songs in their heads: Music and its meaning in children's lives.* New York, NY: Oxford University Press.

Patricia Sheehan Campbell's ethnographic work focuses on the musical culture of the daily lives of American children from very diverse backgrounds. In this text, she explores how these children think about music—their interests, the songs they sing (spontaneous as well as "learned"), the role of music in their everyday activities, and the needs they express for music in their lives. Her narrative account provides strong support for the notion that children have a strong musical culture, which holds significant implications for music educators guiding children in their musical development.

Kohn, A. (1993). *Punished by rewards: The trouble with gold stars, incentive plans, A's, praise, and other bribes.* Boston, MA: Houghton Mifflin.

Alfie Kohn is author of several books on education and parenting, most of which challenge common assumptions about very common practices in American culture. In this book, Kohn challenges the assumption that rewards and incentives (including praise) lead to increased motivation, productivity and quality of work. Rather than "bribing" students to do something in school or punishing them because they do not, Kohn suggests we provide opportunities for collaboration (teamwork) and autonomy (personal choice) that is rooted in meaningful content.

Stake, R., Bresler, L., & Mabry, L. (1991). *Custom and cherishing: The arts in elementary schools.* Urbana, IL: University of Illinois, The Council for Research in Music Education.

This book is a compilation of studies of US elementary school portraying the ordinary problems of teachers teaching music, drama, dance, and the visual arts. The content, pedagogy and leadership of arts education is discussed in relation to six different cases of schools across the United States. Collectively the contents serve as an exemplar for seeing into the "particulars" of issues while simultaneously looking at the "big picture."

Appendix 1
Ethics of Going Into The Field

Every act has potential moral significance, because it is, through its consequences, part of a larger whole of behavior.

John Dewey, *Ethics*, 1932

Action indeed is the sole medium of expression for ethics.

Jane Addams

Getting Oriented

As music teacher educators and authors of *Constructing a Personal Orientation to Music Teaching*, we are strongly grounded in a conception of teacher learning that is informed by practices and methodologies of self-study (Hamilton & Pinnegar, 1998; Ladson-Billings, 1999; Russell & Munby, 1994) and theories of learning in a community (Bruner, 1996; Cochran-Smith & Lytle, 1993; Dewey, 1916). That is, we place significant value on the individual teacher as a primary source of knowledge, reflection, and action. We also place significant value on the importance of learning from others and from learning within different teaching and professional contexts. Furthermore, we believe that being a member of the professional world of music education requires not only the kinds of knowledges and skills obtained in traditional music education degree programs, but sets of knowledges that can only be developed within specific teaching and professional contexts that exist outside of the university. In other words, we see "in the field" experiences as an equal partner with experiences found in the college classroom. Thus, we view music teacher learning and development—whether preservice or inservice—as particularized, situated, and contextualized (Lave & Wenger, 1991; Vygotsky, 1978).

One of our main goals in *Constructing a Personal Orientation to Music Teaching* is to encourage preservice music education teachers to "take to the field" and learn from others. A key requirement for achieving this goal is the active engagement of teachers in inquiry-based learning activities. Although there are many definitions of inquiry-based learning, we see inquiry-based learning in teacher education as the systematic and persistent investigation by a teacher into his or her own teaching and professional environments in order to address problems of practice. For preservice music teachers, inquiry-based learning is an essential component in constructing *knowledge of practice*—knowledge that is personal and practical and based in well thought-out investigations. This knowledge, as Cochran-Smith and Lytle (1993) state, "is constructed collectively within local and broader communities" (p. 271). Thus taking to the field and learning from others serves as an integral part of learning within a community and an important component in becoming an active agent in career-long professional development. Each of the following is an essential knowledge construction site for inquiry-based learning: teaching, learners, curriculum, schools and schooling.

The Ethics of Going into the Field

The advancement of music education could not go forward without systematic inquiries into many aspects of teaching and learning and schools and schooling. Nor could our understanding of the nature of music and learning, and the contexts that characterize and influence both, increase without the generation of new knowledge. However, all investigations—those formally constituted and those less formally organized—are bound by both moral considerations and ethical obligations. Good research, along with good teacher inquiry projects, is marked by certain standards and norms of practice that guide individuals in their actions and judge the conduct of others. In short, a distinguishing marker of a profession is that it is guided by the application of ethics. The healthcare profession is a case in point. Medicine has a long history of being guided and assessing its actions by a code of ethics. Some principles commonly included in the healthcare profession are:

> **Beneficence**—a practitioner should act in the best interest of the patient.
> **Non-malfeasance**—"first, do no harm."
> **Autonomy**—the patient has the right to refuse or choose treatment.
> **Justice**—concerns the distribution of scarce health resources, and the decision of who gets what treatment.

Dignity—the patient (and the person treating the patient) have the right to dignity.

Truthfulness and Honesty—the patient should not be lied to, and deserves to know the whole truth about his or her illness and treatment.

Notice that each principle is value-based and defines the essentials of honorable behavior for individuals in the profession.

Education does not have a "code of ethics" similar to the healthcare profession. For the most part, teachers and schools tend to rely and operate on the values and codes of behavior of the society at large. As the values of and within a society tend to be contested and mediated by conflicting ideologies, a universal set of ethics is too difficult to derive. Yet, if you were to generate a list of values that would likely achieve a high level of consensus and that might act as the ground rules for ethical conduct you might find: trust, honesty, truthfulness, integrity, or acting in good faith. You might also find: respect, dignity and autonomy, tolerance and acceptance, social justice. Or the list might include: responsibility and fairness or caring. Each of these values suggests certain ways of acting and thinking about relations with others. Going into the field and learning from others requires a set of core values to guide our actions. We believe each of the values mentioned above can act as core values in your work in education.

Carrying out your work

There are many kinds of inquiry-based projects in *Constructing a Personal Orientation to Music Teaching*. The most commonly encountered that require human interaction are:

Observational activities
Participatory-interactive studies
Interviews
Shadow studies
School profiles.

The nature and intent of the projects in these books are strictly educational and fall within the boundaries many individuals and institutions would call normal educational practices taking place in accepted educational settings.

Because these studies involve the participation of humans, your college or university's Institutional Review Board (IRB) may need to be consulted before you initiate any one of the projects or activities. Many activities may be exempted from a formal review or may be dealt with in a fairly quick fashion or expedited. But technically, federal law requires that any activity involving the participation of others be subjected to a review process by a group of individuals who oversee and ensure that the activity is managed in a way that is ethical and protects the rights, safety, health and welfare of those who participate in it. The key concern in any data-gathering and reporting project involving people is for the protection of individuals who participate in it. That is, individuals must be willing to participate freely and voluntarily and be informed of all aspects of the project. Individuals must know that they can terminate their participation at any point in a project, without recriminations of any kind.

Because you are a member of a class and the instructor may be giving you an assignment, you probably will not be required to go through any kind of IRB review process. If your institution does require a review process, the responsibility of obtaining permission will most likely fall on the instructors using the text. Regardless of whether a review is required, the safeguards required by the protection of human subjects research laws should guide your work. The three main safeguards are:

Informed consent
Full disclosure about purpose and scope of work
Risk/benefit statement.

Dispositions to Guide Inquiry-based Learning

In all of your work related to the exercises in *Constructing a Personal Orientation to Music Teaching* that involve interactions with individuals, we suggest the following two core dispositions be used as a compass to guide your thinking and actions.

- Generating knowledge that involves *learning from others* is a *privilege* not a right.
- Sensitivity to and respect of the dignity, autonomy, needs, desires, concerns, and legal rights of others is a *responsibility*.

Dispositions are "habits of mind" or ways of being and acting. By assuming and acting with the mindset that we are offered a privilege to learn from others, we honor others and ourselves, plus are afforded freedom. With this honor and freedom comes responsibility, a duty to act in certain ways and be held accountable for our actions.

Appendix 2
How To Use
This Book

Chapter 1. Starting the Journey—Developing a Personal View of Teaching and Learning

Activity Focus	Page	Purpose	Typical Courses and Experiences in Music Teacher Education Program					
			Introduction to Music Education	Methods / Teaching and Learning Class	Practices / Techniques	Practicum / Field Experience	Student Teaching	Graduate course Seminar
TAKE ACTION 1.1: *Connecting to the Past—Powerful Experiences as a Learner*	5	Reflecting on impact of personal learning experiences	☑					☑
TAKE ACTION 1.2: *Connecting to the Past—Powerful Experiences with Music*	6	Reflecting on impact of personal musical experiences	☑	☑				☑
TAKE ACTION 1.3: *Connecting to the Past—Chronology of Educational Musical Experience*	8	Constructing biographical timeline that identifies important musical and educational events	☑					☑

Feature	Description	Page					
TAKE ACTION 1.4: *Successful Teacher / Unsuccessful Teacher*	Identifying and reflecting on successful qualities required for teaching	11	☑	☑		☑	☑
TAKE ACTION 1.5: *Teaching is Like...*	Creating initial personal teaching metaphor	14	☑	☑	☑	☑	☑
TAKE ACTION 1.6: *A Personal Perspective on Teaching and Learning*	Constructing a representation of self as teacher	18	☑	☑	☑	☑	☑
AT CLOSE RANGE 1.1: *Erica: Taking Stock and Looking Forward*	Setting goals	3	☑			☑	
FOCUS ON RESEARCH 1.1: *Influences on Collegiate Students' Decisions to Become a Music Educator*	Influences on career decisions in music education	9	☑				☑
FOCUS ON RESEARCH 1.2: *Gods, Guides, and Gardeners*	Images and metaphors held by preservice teachers	13	☑	☑	☑	☑	☑

Chapter 2. Learning to Teach—From Student to Teacher

Activity Focus	Purpose	Page	Typical Courses and Experiences in Music Teacher Education Program					
			Introduction to Music Education	Methods / Teaching and Learning Class	Practices / Techniques	Practicum / Field Experience	Student Teaching	Graduate course Seminar
TAKE ACTION 2.1: *Gaining Insight from Interviewing Teachers in the Field*	Learning from professional in context	26	☑	☑	☑	☑	☑	☑
TAKE ACTION 2.2: *Examining the Professional Development of Your College Professors*	Learning from experiences of college mentors	27	☑	☑	☑	☑	☑	☑
TAKE ACTION 2.3: *What Concerns Do You have about Music Teaching?*	Articulating concerns and generating learning goals for learning to teach	30	☑	☑	☑	☑	☑	☑
TAKE ACTION 2.4:	Understanding	36	☑	☑	☑	☑	☑	☑

Title	Topic	Page				
Interviewing Student Teachers	concerns during student teaching					
TAKE ACTION 2.5: *Conferencing with Cooperating Teachers*	Understanding professional development	39	☑	☑	☑	
AT CLOSE RANGE 2.1: *Into the Field— Concerns and Goals*	Setting goals	31	☑	☑	☑	☑
AT CLOSE RANGE 2.2: *Emily's First Months of Teaching: Twirling in Circles*	Connecting theory and practice in context	33	☑	☑	☑	☑
FOCUS ON RESEARCH 2.1: *Preservice Music Teachers' Concerns about Teaching*	Teacher development-concerns theory	34		☑	☑	☑

Chapter 3. Learning from Others—Understanding Teacher Career Development

Activity Focus	Purpose	Page	Typical Courses and Experiences in Music Teacher Education Program					
			Introduction to Music Education	Methods / Teaching and Learning Class	Practices / Techniques	Practicum / Field Experience	Student Teaching	Graduate course Seminar
TAKE ACTION 3.1: *Interview a Beginning Teacher*	Gleaning insight into teacher development during the early years	47				☑	☑	☑
TAKE ACTION 3.2: *Looking into the Future*	Becoming aware of personal agency in professional development	51					☑	☑
TAKE ACTION 3.3: *Learn from the Experts*	Analyzing and describing how expertise develops	54		☑	☑		☑	☑
TAKE ACTION 3.4: *Developing Your Expertise from Case Analysis*	Analyzing and describing how expertise develops	55		☑	☑		☑	☑

Chapter 4. Orientations to Teacher Preparation

Activity Focus	Purpose	Page	Typical Courses and Experiences in Music Teacher Education Program					
			Introduction to Music Education	Methods / Teaching and Learning Class	Practices / Techniques	Practicum / Field Experience	Student Teaching	Graduate course Seminar
TAKE ACTION 4.1: *Gaining Insight into Teacher Education: Characterizing Experiences*	Identifying defining attributes and characteristics of teacher education programs	73	☑			☑		☑
TAKE ACTION 4.2: *Gaining Insight into Teacher Education: Your Professors' Perspectives*	Identifying defining attributes and characteristics of teacher education programs	75	☑			☑		☑
TAKE ACTION 4.3: *Gaining Insight into Teacher Education: Analysis of Programs*	Identifying defining attributes and characteristics of the teacher education in which student is enrolled	84	☑			☑		☑

Activity	Objective	Page						
TAKE ACTION 4.4: *Gaining Insight into Teacher Education: Perspectives of Teachers in the Field*	Understanding and evaluating defining attributes and characteristics of teacher education programs	85	☑			☑	☑	☑
TAKE ACTION 4.5: *Gaining Insight into Teacher Education: "In the Driver's Seat"*	Understanding and evaluating defining attributes and characteristics of teacher education programs	87	☑				☑	☑
PROLOGUE 4.1: *Roundtable at the Mentoring Breakfast*	To illustrate theoretical orientations to teacher education	67	☑	☑	☑	☑	☑	☑
FOCUS ON RESEARCH 4.1: *Sex Equity in Music Education*	Awareness of "gender-ness" in music education	80	☑	☑	☑	☑	☑	☑
FOCUS ON RESEARCH 4.2: *Uncovering Preservice Music Teachers' Reflective Thinking*	Awareness of identity and professional development process	82	☑	☑	☑	☑	☑	☑

Chapter 5. Searching for Horizons—Cultivating a Personal Orientation toward Change

Activity Focus	Purpose	Page	Typical Courses and Experiences in Music Teacher Education Program					
			Introduction to Music Education	Methods / Teaching and Learning Class	Practices / Techniques	Practicum / Field Experience	Student Teaching	Graduate course Seminar
TAKE ACTION 5.1: *The Grammars of Schooling and Music Education as You Have Experienced Them*	Uncovering the structural and reproductive nature of schooling	97	☑	☑	☑	☑	☑	☑
TAKE ACTION 5.2: *Less and More for Music Education*	Analyzing curriculum and reform	100	☑	☑	☑	☑	☑	☑
TAKE ACTION 5.3: *Representing a Change Process*	Constructing representation of change process within self	104	☑	☑	☑	☑	☑	☑
TAKE ACTION 5.4: *Becoming a Trend Spotter*	Cultivating disposition of inquiry and renewal	105	☑	☑	☑	☑	☑	☑

Chapter 6. Methodologies for Exploring Teaching and Learning

Activity Focus	Page	Purpose	Typical Courses and Experiences in Music Teacher Education Program					
			Introduction to Music Education	Methods / Teaching and Learning Class	Practices / Techniques	Practicum / Field Experience	Student Teaching	Graduate course Seminar
TAKE ACTION 6.1: *Curriculum Inquiry: Observing with the Commonplaces in Mind*	122	Generating questions for observations, reflections and deliberations on curriculum concerns		☑	☑	☑	☑	☑
TAKE ACTION 6.2: *The Criteria of Scholars —And Your Musical Experiences*	125	Reflecting on and deducing how criteria are used in teaching and learning		☑	☑	☑	☑	☑
TAKE ACTION 6.3: *Curriculum Deliberations*	129	Broadening awareness of curriculum images and their intents	☑	☑	☑	☑	☑	☑

Chapter 6. *Continued*

		Typical Courses and Experiences in Music Teacher Education Program					
		Introduction to Music Education	Methods / Teaching and Learning Class	Practices / Techniques	Practicum / Field Experience	Student Teaching	Graduate course Seminar
overlapping realms of work							
TAKE ACTION 6.9 *Developmental Portfolio* Creating a portfolio that reflects personal development and growth in becoming a student of teaching	159					☑	☑
AT CLOSE RANGE 6.1: *A Tale of Two Schools* Illustrates contrasting school cultures	144	☑	☑	☑	☑	☑	
AT CLOSE RANGE 6.2 *The Philosophy of an Intermediate School as an Invitation for School Study* Illustrates relationships between mission, teacher actions, and students' experiences	152		☑				☑

FOCUS ON RESEARCH	Description	Page						
FOCUS ON RESEARCH 6.1: *Seeing and Hearing Music Teaching and Learning*	Ethnography and portraiture as research approaches for teachers	131	☑		☑			☑
FOCUS ON RESEARCH 6.2: *Diva Irina: An English Language Learner in High School Choir*	Description of a student's perspective of music learning in high school	144	☑	☑	☑	☑	☑	☑
FOCUS ON RESEARCH 6.3: *An Exploratory Investigation of Three Middle School General Music Students' Beliefs About Music Education* (Wayman), and *The Meaning of Music Education to Middle School General Music Students* ([Wayman] Davis)	Two studies coupled to illustrate the beliefs and perspectives of students' music learning in middle school	145	☑	☑	☑	☑	☑	☑
FOCUS ON RESEARCH 6.4: *Looking at Schools as Musical Cultures*	Illustrates the sonic environment of an elementary school	149	☑	☑	☑	☑	☑	

Notes

1 Richardson and Placier based their explanation of teacher change models on the work of Chin and Benne (1969).
2 You may want to compare this list with the National Standards in Music Education.
3 See the School District Demographics System (US Department of Education Institute of Education Sciences, 2008; http://nces.ed.gov/surveys/sdds/index.asp) or the Great Schools Network (http://www.greatschools.net/).
4 "Northshore" is a pseudonym for the school, following the Human Subjects guidelines to protect the anonymity of participants in a research study in preparation by one of the authors. The data cited in this chapter are not part of the research project.

References

Archambault, R. D. (Ed.). (1964). *John Dewey on education: Selected writings.* Chicago, IL: University of Chicago Press.

Ayers, W. (2001). *To teach: The journey of a teacher.* New York, NY: Teachers College Press.

Barresi, A., & Albrecht, G. (2000). School culture. In G. B. Olson, J. R. Barrett, N. S. Rasmussen, A. Barresi & J. Jensen (Eds.), *Looking in on music teaching* (pp. 119–131). New York, NY: Primis/McGraw-Hill.

Barrett, J. R. (2005). Planning for understanding: A reconceptualized view of the music curriculum. *Music Educators Journal, 91*(4), 21–25.

Barrett, J. R. (Ed.). (2009). *Music education at a crossroads: Realizing the goal of music for all.* Lanham, MD: Rowman & Littlefield Education.

Barrett, J. R., McCoy, C. W., & Veblen, K. K. (1997). *Sound ways of knowing: Music in the interdisciplinary curriculum.* New York, NY: Schirmer Books.

Barrett, J. R., & Rasmussen, N. S. (1996). What observation reveals: Videotaped cases as windows to preservice teachers' beliefs about music teaching and learning. *Bulletin of the Council for Research in Music Education, 130,* 75–88.

Bartel, L. R. (Ed.). (2004). *Questioning the music education paradigm.* Waterloo, Canada: Canadian Music Educators' Association.

Bergee, M. J., Coffman, D. D., Demorest, S. M., Humphreys, J. T., & Thornton, L. P. (2001). Influences on collegiate students' decision to become a music educator. Retrieved from http://www.menc.org/networks/rnc/Bergee-Report.html

Bergee, M. J., & Grashel, J. W. (2002). Relationship of generalized self-efficacy, career decisiveness, and general teacher efficacy to preparatory music teachers' professional self-efficacy. *Missouri Journal of Research in Music Education, 39*, 4–20.

Berliner, D. C. (1994). Expertise: The world of exemplary performances. In J. N. Mangieri & C. C. Block (Eds.), *Creating powerful thinking in teachers and students* (pp. 161–186). Fort Worth, TX: Holt, Rinehart, and Winston.

Boardman, E. (1985). Teacher education: A wedding of theory and practice. *Bulletin of the Council for Research in Music Education, 81*, 65–73.

Boardman, E. (1992). New environments for teacher education. *Music Educators Journal, 79*(2), 41–43.

Boardman, E. (Ed.). (2002). *Dimensions of musical learning and teaching: A different kind of classroom.* Reston, VA: MENC: The National Association for Music Education.

Borich, G. D. (2000). *Effective teaching methods* (4th ed.). Upper Saddle River, NJ: Prentice Hall/Pearson Education.

Bowers, J. (1997). Sequential patterns and the music teaching effectiveness of elementary education majors. *Journal of Research in Music Education, 45*(3), 428–443.

Brand, M. (2002). The love of music is not enough. *Music Educators Journal, 88*(5), 45–46, 53.

Bresler, L. (1998). The genre of school music and its shaping by meso, micro, and macro contexts. *Research Studies in Music Education, 11*, 2–18.

Bruner, J. (1996). *The culture of education.* Cambridge, MA: Harvard University Press.

Bullough, R. V., Jr. (1989). *First-year teacher: A case study.* New York, NY: Teachers College Press.

Bullough, R. V., Jr., & Baughman, K. (1997). *"First-year teacher" eight years later: An inquiry into teacher development.* New York, NY: Teachers College Press.

Bullough, R. V., Jr., Holt, L., & Goddstein, S. L. (1984) *Human interests in the curriculum: Teaching and learning in a technological society.* New York, NY: Teachers College Press.

Bullough, R. V., Jr., & Gitlin, A. D. (2001). *Becoming a student of teaching: Linking knowledge production and practice* (2nd ed.). New York, NY: RoutledgeFalmer.

Bullough, R. V., Jr., & Stokes, D. K. (1994). Analyzing personal teaching metaphors in preservice teacher education as a means for encouraging professional development. *American Educational Research Journal, 31*(1), 197–224.

Burke, J., & Krajicek, J. (2006). *Letters to a new teacher: A month-by-month guide to the year ahead.* Portsmouth, NH: Heinemann.

Burke, P. J., & McDonnell, J. H. (1992). Enthusiastic and growing. In R. Fessler & J. C. Christensen (Eds.), *Teacher career cycle: Understanding and guiding the professional development of teachers* (pp. 119–151). Needham Heights, MA: Allyn & Bacon.

Campbell, M. R. (1999). Learning to teach music: A collaborative ethnography. *Bulletin of the Council for Research in Music Education, 139*, 12–36.

Campbell, M. R. (Ed.). (2007). Music teacher education special focus issue. *Music Educators Journal, 93*(3).

Campbell, M. R., & Brummett, V. M. (2002). Professional teaching portfolios: For pros and preservice teachers alike. *Music Educators Journal, 89*(2), 25–30, 57.

Campbell, M. R., & Burdell, P. A. (1996). Conceptions of knowledge and teaching practice among music education students and elementary education students. *McGill Journal of Education, 31*(3), 231–245.

Campbell, M. R., & Thompson, L. K. (2001). *Preservice music educators' images of teaching.* Paper presented at the Desert Skies Symposium on Research in Music Education, Tucson, AZ.

Campbell, M. R., & Thompson, L. K. (2007). Perceived concerns of preservice music education teachers: A cross-sectional study. *Journal of Research in Music Education, 55*(2), 162–176.

Campbell, P. S. (1998). *Songs in their heads: Music and its meaning in children's lives.* New York, NY: Oxford University Press.

Carlow, R. (2006). Diva Irina: An English language learner in high school choir. *Bulletin of the Council for Research in Music Education, 170,* 63–77.

Carter, K., & Anders, D. (1996). Program pedagogy. In F. B. Murray (Ed.), *The teacher educator's handbook: Building a knowledge base for the preparation of teachers* (pp. 557–592). San Francisco, CA: Jossey-Bass.

Chin, R., & Benne, K. (1969). General strategies for effecting changes in human systems. In W. Bennis, K. Benne, & R. Chin (Eds.), *The planning of change* (2nd ed., pp. 32–59). New York, NY: Holt, Rinehart, Winston.

Cochran-Smith, M., & Lytle, S. L. (1993). *Inside/outside: Teacher research and knowledge.* New York, NY: Teachers College Press.

Conkling, S. W. (2003). Uncovering preservice music teachers' reflective thinking: Making sense of learning to teach. *Bulletin of the Council for Research in Music Education, 155,* 11–23.

Conkling, S. W., & Henry, W. (1999). Professional development partnerships: A new model for music teacher preparation. *Arts Education Policy Review, 100*(4), 19–23.

Cutietta, R. A., & Thompson, L. K. (2000). Voices of experience speak on music teaching. *Music Educators Journal, 87*(3), 40–43, 51.

Davis, V. W. (2009). The meaning of music education to middle school general music students. *Bulletin of the Council for Research in Music Education, 179,* 61–77.

Delpit, L. (1995). *Other people's children: Cultural conflict in the classroom.* New York, NY: New Press.

Dewey, J. (1904). The relation of theory to practice in the education of teachers. In C. McMurry (Ed.), *The third yearbook of the National Society for the Scientific Study of Education, Part I* (pp. 9–30). Chicago, IL: University of Chicago Press.

Dewey, J. (1916). *Democracy and education.* New York, NY: Macmillan.

Dewey, J. (1922). *Human nature and conduct: An introduction to social psychology.* New York, NY: H. Holt.

Dewey, J. (1932). *Ethics.* New York, NY: Holt.

Dewey, J. (1934). *Art as experience.* New York, NY: Perigee.

Dewey, J. (1938). *Experience and education.* New York, NY: Collier Books.

Duke, R. A. (1999). Measures of instructional effectiveness in music research. *Bulletin of the Council for Research in Music Education, 143,* 1–48.

Duke, R. A. (2005). *Intelligent music teaching: Essays on the core principles of effective instruction.* Austin, TX: Learning and Behavior Resources.

Eisner, E. (2002). *The arts and the creation of mind.* New Haven, CT: Yale University Press.

Eisner, E. W. (1985). *The educational imagination: On the design and evaluation of school programs.* New York, NY: Macmillan.

Emerson, R. W. (1860/1876). Illusions from the "Conduct of Life". *The collected works of Ralph Waldo Emerson: The conduct of life* (Vol. VI). Cambridge, MA: Harvard University Press.

Feiman-Nemser, S. (1990). Teacher education: Structural and conceptual alternatives. In W. R. Houston (Ed.), *Handbook of research on teacher education* (pp. 212–223). New York, NY: Macmillan.

Feiman-Nemser, S. (2001). From preparation to practice: Designing a continuum to strengthen and sustain teaching. *Teachers College Record, 103*(6), 1013–1055.

Fessler, R. (1992). Teacher career cycle. In R. Fessler & J. C. Christensen (Eds.), *Teacher career cycle: Understanding and guiding the professional development of teachers* (pp. 21–44). Needham Heights, MA: Allyn & Bacon.

Frede, E. (2003). How teachers grow: Four stages. *High/Scope Resources*, 21–22.

Frierson-Campbell, C. (Ed.). (2006). *Teaching music in the urban classroom: A guide to survival, success, and reform* (Vol. 1). Lanham, MD: Rowman & Littlefield.

Frierson-Campbell, C. (2007). Without the 'ism: Thoughts about equity and social justice in music education. *Music Education Research, 9*(2), 255–265.

Fullan, M. (2007). *The new meaning of educational change* (4th ed.). New York, NY: Teachers College Press.

Fuller, F. (1969). Concerns of teachers: A developmental conceptualization. *American Educational Research Journal, 6*, 207–226.

Fuller, F. F., & Bown, O. H. (1975). Becoming a teacher. In K. Ryan (Ed.), *Teacher education (The seventy-fourth yearbook of the National Society for the Study of Education)*. Chicago, IL: University of Chicago Press.

Furlong, J., & Maynard, T. (1995). *Mentoring student teachers: The growth of professional knowledge*. London, England: Routledge.

Gardner, H. (2004). *Changing minds: The art and science of changing our own and other people's minds*. Boston, MA: Harvard Business School Press.

Greene, M. (1995). *Releasing the imagination: Essays on education, the arts, and social change*. San Francisco, CA: Jossey-Bass.

Greene, M. (2001). *Variations on a blue guitar: The Lincoln Center Institute lectures on aesthetic education*. New York, NY: Teachers College Press.

Guillaume, A. M., & Rudney, G. L. (1993). Student teachers' growth toward independence: An analysis of their changing concerns. *Teaching and Teacher Education, 9*(1), 65–80.

Hall, G. E., Wallace, R. C., & Dossett, W. A. (1973). *A developmental conceptualization of the adoption process within educational institutions (Rep No. 3006)*. Austin, TX: University of Texas at Austin, The Research and Development Center for Teacher Education.

Hamilton, M. L., & Pinnegar, S. (1998). Conclusions: The value and the promise of self-study. In M. L. Hamilton (Ed.), *Reconceptualizing teaching practice: Self-study in teacher education* (pp. 235–246). Bristol, PA: Falmer Press.

Hammerness, K. (2006). *Seeing through teachers' eyes: Professional ideals and classroom practice*. New York, NY: Teachers College Press.

Hargreaves, A. (1994). *Changing teachers, changing times: Teachers' work and culture in the postmodern age*. New York, NY: Teachers College Press.

Hargreaves, A. (1998). The emotional practice of teaching. *Teaching and Teacher Education, 14*(8), 835–854.

Hargreaves, A. (2005). Educational change takes ages: Life, career and generational factors in teachers' emotional responses to educational change. *Teaching and Teacher Education, 21*(8), 967–983.

Hargreaves, A., & Fink, D. (2006). *Sustainable leadership*. San Francisco, CA: Jossey-Bass.

Hendel, C. (1995). Behavioral characteristics and instructional patterns of selected music teachers. *Journal of Research in Music Education, 43*(3), 182–203.

Howey, K. R., & Zimpher, N. L. (1989). *Profiles of preservice teacher education: Inquiry into the nature of programs*. Albany, NY: State University of New York Press.

Huberman, M. (1989). On teachers' careers: Once over lightly, with a broad brush. *International Journal of Education Research, 13*, 347–362.

Huberman, M. (1992). Teacher development and instructional mastery. In A. Hargreaves & M. G. Fullan (Eds.), *Understanding teacher development* (pp. 122–142). New York, NY: Teachers College Press.

Huberman, M. (1993). *The lives of teachers* (J. Neufeld, Trans.). New York, NY: Teachers College Press.

Ingersoll, R. M. (2001). Teacher turnover and teacher shortages: An organizational analysis. *American Educational Research Journal, 38*, 499–534.

Interstate New Teacher Assessment and Support Consortium. The interstate new teacher and support consortium (INTASC) teacher standards. Retrieved from http://www.ccsso.org/projects/Interstate_New_Teacher_Assessment_and_Support_Consortium/

Johnson, L. (1992). *Dangerous minds.* New York, NY: St. Martin's Press.

Jorgensen, E. R. (1997). *In search of music education.* Urbana, IL: University of Illinois Press.

Jorgensen, E. R. (2003). *Transforming music education.* Indianapolis, IN: Indiana University Press.

Jorgensen, E. R. (2007). Concerning justice and music education. *Music Education Research, 9*(2), 169–189.

Joseph, P. B., & Burnaford, G. E. (Eds.). (2001). *Images of schoolteachers in America* (2nd ed.). Mahwah, NJ: Lawrence Erlbaum.

Kane, P. R. (Ed.). (1996). *My first year as a teacher.* New York, NY: Signet.

Katz, L. (1992). Early childhood programs: Multiple perspectives on quality. *Childhood Education, 69*, 66–71.

Kennedy, M. M. (2005). *Inside teaching: How classroom life undermines reform.* Cambridge, MA: Harvard University Press.

Kidder, T. (1990). *Among schoolchildren.* New York, NY: Harper Perennial.

Kimpton, J. (2005). What to do about music teacher education: Our profession at a crossroads. *Journal of Music Teacher Education, 14*(2), 8–21.

Kliebard, H. (1972). Metaphorical roots of curriculum design. *Teachers College Record, 72*(3), 403–404.

Kohn, A. (1993). *Punished by rewards: The trouble with gold starts, incentive plans, A's, praise, and other bribes.* Boston, MA: Houghton Mifflin.

Koza, J. E. (1993). Big boys don't cry (or sing): Gender, misogyny, and homophobia in college choral methods texts. *The Quarterly Journal of Music Teaching and Learning, IV*(4), 48–64.

Kratus, J. (2007). Music education at the tipping point. *Music Educators Journal, 94*(2), 42–48.

Ladson-Billings, G. (1999). Preparing teachers for diverse student populations: A critical race theory perspective. In A. Irna-Nejad & P. Pearson (Eds.), *Review of research in education* (Vol. 24, pp. 211–247). Washington, DC: American Educational Research Association.

Lakoff, G., & Johnson, M. (1980). *Metaphors we live by.* Chicago, IL: University of Chicago Press.

Langer, S. K. (1942). *Philosophy in a new key: A study in the symbolism of reason, rite, and art.* Boston, MA: Oxford University Press.

Lave, J., & Wenger, E. (1991). *Situated learning: Legitimate peripheral participation.* Cambridge, United Kingdom: Cambridge University Press.

Lawrence-Lightfoot, S., & Davis, J. H. (1997). *The art and science of portraiture.* San Francisco, CA: Jossey-Bass.

Lieberman, A., & Miller, L. (Eds.). (2001). *Teachers caught in the act: Professional development that matters.* New York, NY: Teachers College Press.

Lortie, D. C. (2002). *Schoolteacher: A sociological study* (2nd ed.). Chicago, IL: University of Chicago Press.

Lum, C.-H., & Campbell, P. S. (2007). The sonic surrounds of an elementary school. *Journal of Research in Music Education, 55*(1), 31–47.

Mark, M. L., & Gary, C. L. (2007). *A history of American music education* (3rd ed.). Lanham, MD: Rowman & Littlefield Education.

Miller, P. C. (Ed.). (2004). *Narratives from the classroom: An introduction to teaching.* Thousand Oaks, CA: Sage Publications.

Miranda, M. L., Robbins, J., & Stauffer, S. L. (2007). Seeing and hearing music teaching and learning: Transforming classroom observations through ethnography and portraiture. *Research Studies in Music Education, 28*(1), 3–21.

Mumford, L. (1951). *The conduct of life.* New York, NY: Harcourt Brace.

National Board of Professional Teaching Standards. Music standards of the national board of professional teaching standards (NBPTS). Retrieved from http://www.nbpts.org/the_standards/standards_by_cert?ID=14&x=40&y=9

O'Toole, P. (1993). I sing in a choir but I have "no voice!" *The Quarterly Journal of Music Teaching and Learning, IV*(4), 65–76.

Office of Human Subjects Research (2009). National Institutes of Health, from http://ohsr.od.nih.gov/guidelines/belmont.html

Olson, G. B., Barrett, J. R., Rasmussen, N. S., Barresi, A., & Jensen, J. (2000). *Looking in on music teaching.* New York, NY: Primis/McGraw-Hill.

Ortega y Gasset, J. (1942). *Meditations on Quixote.* Buenos Aires, Argentina: Espasa-Caipe.

Patton, M. Q. (1990). *Qualitative evaluation and research methods.* Newbury Park, CA: Sage Publications.

Posner, G. J. (2004). *Field experience: A guide to reflective teaching* (6th ed.). New York, NY: Allyn & Bacon.

Raths, J. (1999). A consumer's guide to teacher standards. *Phi Delta Kappan, 81*(2), 136–142.

Reimer, B. (1991). Criteria for quality in music. In R. A. Smith & A. Simpson (Eds.), *Aesthetics and arts education* (pp. 330–338). Urbana, IL: University of Illinois Press.

Reimer, B. (2007). Roots of inequity and injustice: The challenges for music education. *Music Education Research, 9*(2), 191–204.

Richardson, V., & Placier, P. (2001). Teacher change. In V. Richardson (Ed.), *Handbook of research on teaching* (4th ed., pp. 905–947). Washington, DC: American Educational Research Association.

Rose, M. (1995). *Possible lives: The promise of public education in America.* New York, NY: Penguin Books.

Russell, T., & Munby, H. (1994). The authority of experience in learning to teach: Messages from a physics case. *Journal of Teacher Education, 45*(2), 86–96.

Samaras, A. P., & Freese, A. R. (2006). *Self-study of teaching practices: Primer.* New York, NY: Peter Lang.

Sarason, S. B. (1971). *The culture of the school and the problem of change* (2nd ed.). Boston, MA: Allyn and Bacon.

Sarason, S. B. (1993). *The case for change: Rethinking the preparation of educators.* San Francisco, CA: Jossey-Bass.

Schimmels, C. (1985). *I was a high school drop in.* Grand Rapids, MI: Revell.

Schön, D. A. (1983). *The reflective practitioner: How professionals think in action.* New York, NY: Basic Books.

Schön, D. A. (1987). *Educating the reflective practitioner.* San Francisco, CA: Jossey-Bass.

Schoonmaker, F. (2002). *Growing up teaching: From personal knowledge to professional practice.* New York, NY: Teachers College Press.

Schubert, W. H. (1986). *Curriculum: Perspective, paradigm, and possibility.* New York, NY: Macmillan.

Schwab, J. J. (1954/1978). Eros and education: A discussion of one aspect of discussion. In I. Westbury & N. Wilkof (Eds.), *Science, curriculum and liberal education: Selected essays* (pp. 105–132). Chicago, IL: University of Chicago Press.

Schwab, J. J. (1959/1978). The "impossible" role of the teacher in progressive education. In I. Westbury & N. Wilkof (Eds.), *Science, curriculum and liberal education: Selected essays* (pp. 167–183). Chicago, IL: University of Chicago Press.

Schwab, J. J. (1983). The practical 4: Something for curriculum professors to do. *Curriculum Inquiry, 13*(3), 239–265.

Sedlak, M. W. (1987). Tomorrow's teachers: The essential arguments of the Holmes Group report. *Teachers College Record, 88*(3), 314–325.

Stake, R., Bresler, L., & Mabry, L. (1991). *Custom and cherishing: The arts in elementary schools.* Urbana, IL: University of Illinois: The Council for Research in Music Education.

Stevenson, C. (1998). *Teaching ten to fourteen year olds* (2nd ed.). White Plains, NY: Longman.

Taba, H. (1962). *Curriculum development: Theory and practice.* New York, NY: Harcourt, Brace, and World.

Thiessen, D., & Anderson, A. (1999). *Getting into the habit of change in Ohio schools: The cross-case study of 12 transforming learning communities.* Columbus, OH: Ohio Department of Education.

Thiessen, D., & Barrett, J. R. (2002). Reform-minded music teachers: A more comprehensive image of teaching for music teacher education. In R. Colwell & C. Richardson (Eds.), *New handbook of research on music teaching and learning* (pp. 759–785). New York, NY: Oxford University Press.

Thomas, R. B. (1971). *MMCP synthesis: One of the major products of the Manhattanville Music Curriculum Program.* Elnora, NY: Media.

Thompson, L. K. (2000). *Freshman music education majors' preconceived beliefs about the people and processes involved in teaching.* Unpublished doctoral dissertation, University of Arizona, Tucson.

Thompson, L. K., & Campbell, M. R. (2005). Guides, gods, and gardeners: Preservice music education students' personal teaching metaphors. *Bulletin of the Council for Research in Music Education, 158,* 43–54.

Tyack, D., & Cuban, L. (1995). *Tinkering toward Utopia: A century of public school reform.* Cambridge, MA: Harvard University Press.

U.S. Department of Education: National Center for Education Statistics (2008). Digest of Education Statistics. Retrieved from http://nces.ed.gov/fastfacts/display.asp?id=84

Vygotsky, L. (1978). *Mind in society* (M. Cole, Trans.). Cambridge, MA: Harvard University Press.

Walker, D. F. (2003). *Fundamentals of curriculum: Passion and professionalism* (2nd ed.). Mahwah, NJ: Lawrence Erlbaum.

Walker, D. F., & Soltis, J. F. (2004). *Curriculum and aims* (4th ed.). New York, NY: Teachers College Press.

Wallis, C., & Steptoe, C. (2006, December 18). How to bring our schools out of the 20th century. *Time, 168,* 50–56.

Wayman, V. E. (2004). An exploratory investigation of three middle school general music students' beliefs about music education. *Bulletin of the Council for Research in Music Education, 160,* 26–37.

Weaver, M. A. (1993). A survey of big ten institutions: Gender distinctions regarding faculty ranks and salaries in schools, divisions, and departments of music. *The Quarterly Journal of Music Teaching and Learning, IV*(4), 92–99.

Williams, D. A. (2007). What are music educators doing and how well are we doing it? *Music Educators Journal, 94*(1), 18–23.

Wong, H. K., & Wong, R. T. (1998). *The first days of school: How to be an effective teacher.* Mountain View, CA: Harry K. Wong.

Woodford, P. G. (2005). *Democracy and music education: Liberalism, ethics, and the politics of practice.* Bloomington, IN: Indiana University Press.

Yarbrough, C., & Price, H. E. (1989). Sequential patterns of instruction in music. *Journal of Research in Music Education, 37*(3), 179–187.

Zemelman, S., Daniels, H., & Hyde, A. (2005). *Best practice: Today's standards for teaching and learning in America's schools.* Portsmouth, NH: Heinemann.

Index